Representatives Become Rulers

A Blue Collar Perspective of Government Behaviors

Randy Miller

Randy-miller.blogspot.com
Rlmiller1@comcast.net

authorHOUSE®

AuthorHouse™
1663 Liberty Drive
Bloomington, IN 47403
www.authorhouse.com
Phone: 1-800-839-8640

First published by AuthorHouse 6/7/2010

ISBN: 978-1-4520-0727-4 (e)
ISBN: 978-1-4520-0725-0 (sc)
ISBN: 978-1-4520-0726-7 (hc)

Library of Congress Control Number: 2010904828

Printed in the United States of America
Bloomington, Indiana

This book is printed on acid-free paper.

Table of Contents

Introduction

I have often wondered why the majority of Americans, Blue Collar everyday working people struggling to make it from week to week and month to month, trying to raise families in difficult economic times, are able to recognize the real issues and ask the right questions, which always go unasked and unanswered, because the politicians give no credence to the people they are elected to serve.

Will we ever reach a day where the American People become a special interest? And if so what will it take to bring it about? Is there cause to worry when a political slogan such as "The Peoples' Seat" becomes the uncharacteristic winner? My question then becomes; aren't all of the seats the "Peoples' Seat?" According to the Constitution they are; so just who is it that took them away from us?

This started out to be a book about Earmarks, Waste, Abuse and Fraud in our government spending. I started out trying to understand where we lost the stewardship over our money; but soon was questioning; when did we lose the stewardship of our ideas of proper representation to the politicians? How our politicians began to serve their own interests instead of the interests of the ones who put them in office. What happened to morals and ethics in government?

John 15:20
Most assuredly I say to you,
A servant is not greater than his master;
Nor is he who is sent,
greater than he who sent him.

So who works for whom in this political process of ours. The Founding Fathers defined political positions to be an opportunity to serve the needs of the country. They never anticipated that it would become a profession, positions which elected officials would hold for years and years, be paid handsomely for their service and would replace the needs of their country with their own.. Nor did they define the success of the politician to be how much each would be able to steal from the Treasury and divert to their own interests. This is a justification by current day politicians of their abuse, theft and fraud perpetrated on the American people.

I think we are in dangerous territory when we accept behavior from our politicians that we wouldn't accept from our own children. When a Senator like Christopher Dodd can stand before a Television camera and intentionally lie to us about his actions and then when caught tells us it is really okay that he did it; or a politician like John Murtha can steal over $150,000,000 of our money for his own little used airport, named after himself, that services less than 10,000 passengers per year, not to mention the Billions of dollars he has stolen from our Treasury to fulfill his own personal opinions of what our militaries need even when they say they don't want it; we have serious problems that we are going to have to face as citizens.

What does it say about the attitude in Washington D.C. when Rep. Eric Massas of New York states on national television that it doesn't matter what his constituents say or think when it comes to his vote? If he feels personally that his opinion is better than that of the people he represents and he will vote his opinion and Constituents be damned!.

Then there is Sen. Thomas Carper (D) Delaware, who sits on the committee crafting the Healthcare Reform bill before the Senate, when questioned about the length of the bill and whether he had read it, replied; "…it is full of arcane gibberish…I don't expect to actually read the legislative language, because reading the legislative language is among the more confusing things I've ever read in my life."[1]

Our politicians continually prove they are not to be trusted to do what is right or to exercise proper stewardship over our Treasury so it will have to come from us. Until we choose to get serious about the

---

1 CNSNews.com – Townhall Magazine Nov issue HamNation – Mary Katharine Ham

power of our vote and hold responsible those legislators who continually display this miscreant behavior by removing them from office there is little hope for change.

The time has come to let the "Truth" set them free! Free to pursue work in the private sector because the truth is that history proves the "professional politician," by most accounts, is incapable of putting the interests of the country before their own interests.

Imagine if you can, had people like John Murtha and Ted Stevens been removed at the first sign of their personal arrogance, how many billions of wasted dollars could we have saved? What about Rep. Bobby Rush from Chicago and the $305,500 he earmarked for the church he founded and where he pursues his work as an ordained minister? Would your church be thrilled to receive that kind of manna from Heaven? How do you feel about contributing to his personal self serving charity? I guess it is true that charity begins at home!

Who signed us up for this marathon race of spending? Just how dangerous is the concept of spending our way out of bankruptcy? How much longer will we accept the notion that continual abuse of taxpayer dollars to finance pet projects and campaign supporter debts by our politicians and their continual resistance of transparency is acceptable behavior?

When I began my research for this book we weren't yet in the banking and auto businesses. We hadn't yet found ourselves exposed to the liability of 23 trillion dollars plus in government provided bailout money and loan guarantees that the TARP Bill has now exposed us to.

My original intention was to question the waste and self interest of how our money is spent, but I soon found myself overwhelmed by so many examples of blatant disregard for *"integrity, honesty and morality"* that it began to take on a *new flavor, that, when looked at in its totality, takes on a very sour odor and taste.* Maybe this is the swine smell that Sen. Harkin is so worried about. From a single vote being bought for 3.5 billion dollars by one member to sleight of hand that created a billion dollar earmark in the stimulus bill for construction of a plant that studies show is obsolete before the shovel hits the dirt they continually make decisions that protect their own self interests.

It is a new game now and more important than ever that we require our government to go through our budget line by line, a campaign guarantee by candidate Obama, and remove waste, duplicative spending and expenditures that deny open debate and eliminate the dubious practice of *"off budget"* expenditures such as the cost of the war. The money we are spending is not *"Monopoly Money,"* it is real money, it is our money and it is our right not only to demand a full accounting but also to assure that our money be spent for the *"good of our society as a whole" regardless of whether it is on or off budget expenditures.* Why do we have "off budget" expenditures?

The 2008 election was sold as a mandate by the voters for change in the way we are governed. The perception was that walls were going to be erected around Washington D.C. that would prevent the old ways from infecting the new. Unfortunately the Stimulus Bill proved to be the first example that this wall was built of Styrofoam not cement as Chapter 5 "In his Own Words" would have us believe.

To be sure it is way too early to give up on our hope for this change. But some concern should be felt about the accomplishments so far. It is not every politician that has fallen victim to the sense of arrogance and entitlement but they are surely in the minority and until they become the majority there is little hope for change.

Some of these politicians are so blatant in their actions, so outspoken in their belief they are above the law and so resistant to *"transparency"* that they are deserving of their own chapters. At the same time I tried to give praise to those few who actually are dedicated in their efforts to expose those who have no compunction with stealing our taxpayer dollars for their own self aggrandizement and job security.

I have included numerous samples of pork barrel spending from both the supposedly *pork free* Stimulus Bill and from the fiscal year 2009 budget. Obviously if all were included in this book it would create a book to heavy to pickup so what I have tried to do to keep it manageable is to include some of what I will call my favorites. But trust me you will come away with a sense of total confusion as to how anybody could justify, in their own mind, let alone defend in public debate, the value and importance of these expenditures. You will see that for the majority of them the real purpose is nothing more than to use our money as the capital they use to payback their own political debts to supporters and contributors or use to protect their incumbencies in their next election.

I have broken the examples into sections such as "Forget Waldo, see if you can find the jobs!" Hopefully my attempts to use humor and sarcasm with these examples will help you to keep your blood pressure down. I found that this was my biggest challenge as I discovered new and unbelievable behavior.

The questions I am asking and the behaviors I point out are not so complicated as to require a PHD in Economics or Finance or require long legalese filled answers. They are simple down to earth questions we have every right to expect our politicians to ask on our behalf.

1. Why do we have *"on budget"* and *"off budget"* categories?
2. Why do politicians resist the notion of *"transparency?"*
3. When did a *"Billion dollars"* become such a trivial amount as to not be worth the effort of saving?
4. Was it a mistake to allow our system of governing to become *"a profession rather than an opportunity to serve?"*
5. Why do we continually accept the *"Hypocrisy"* as an accepted form of governing?
6. Exactly who is it that says we have to accept *"Pork Barrel and Earmark"* spending?
7. If Rep. John Murtha really knows more about the needs of our armed forces than the Dept. of Defense then why don't we just close down the Pentagon?
8. Isn't it pretty obvious why almost all defense Contractors maintain, at the very least, an office in Rep. Murthas' home state of Pennsylvania?
9. Are *"Honesty and Integrity"* an unreasonable expectation of our elected officials?
10. Is it time for reform in the Ethics committees so that theft of the Treasury, tax evasion and paybacks to special interests no longer goes unpunished?
11. We spend millions of dollars each year on farming subsidies for farmers to not raise crops or to cut the sizes of their dairy cattle herds in an effort to reduce production and control prices; so

why do our food banks cry out every day for needed donations from the public?

In the latter half of the 19th and first half of the 20th century "Robber Barons" were the leaders of the railroads, oil and steel companies. In the 21st century it is our elected politicians who have become the "Robber Barons." We couldn't vote them out when they were in private business but this new evolving species should be eradicated as quickly as we would eradicate a non native fish or plant. Maybe poison would be the best and quickest, it works on fish!

I hope that you too will be amazed by their brazen conduct and left with similar feelings of disappointment and anger as I at how little we actually mean to so many of our elected leaders.

I have also discovered in my research that there are a lot of nonprofit organizations that are truly trying to change the behavior of government and I hope that you will see the need, as I did, to offer your support.

Chapter 1

The Anatomy of a Vote

The power of our vote is an encumbrance, put upon us by our founding fathers in the belief that it would assure the powers of the government remain in the hands of the governed. Much heavier than a right, it is a responsibility not given to just the richest or the smartest, it is encumbered on all equally. But the one true action we can take to shape our government to the wills of the people seems to be infected with a complacency whose origins appear born by a feeling of futility. The notion or belief that the behaviors of our representatives, based on past performance, are so hopelessly embedded in our system that the power is gone from our vote. But the truth is;

> "Bad officials are elected by good citizens who don't vote."
> George Jean Nathan

Defined as "giving an indication of approval or disapproval of a proposal, motion or candidate for office,"[2] our vote can still carry the power of change, it can still shape the government desired by the governed if we only commit to its use and be a part of the process.

Implied Expectations

When we cast our vote for a candidate there is a weight of implied expectation that he or she will govern in the interest of the country as a whole, will exercise stewardship over our resources and conduct

---

2   Merriam Webster Collegiate Dictionary

themselves with honesty, integrity and morality. If these expectations go unmet the result is Rulers not Representative's.

> Nothing is politically right which is morally wrong."
> Attributed to Daniel O'Connell

When a member states that it is his decision how he will vote on an issue regardless of the expectations of his constituents, or they stand before the people and lie, call the citizens attending town meetings un-American or Nazi's for their outbursts and imply that the rhetoric of the people is nothing more than an approval for assassination, it should become clear to all of us that we have a problem and its only solution is the power of the vote.

The vote is our power to shape the makeup and direction of our country in such a way that it adheres to the will of the people, operates on the values that we find most important and protects personal rights and freedoms from the neediest to the wealthiest. But all too often those we send to represent us fall victim to the competition for power, dollars and personal gain. Their concern becomes what they can misappropriate for their enrichment and the enrichment of their political supporters. Shedding the title of Representative we have placed upon them, they choose instead to anoint themselves as Ruler. They are all too often, (read Charlie Rangel here) allowed to live outside the law which the rest of us are governed by.

So just who owns the votes they cast?

To not match the use of their vote in governing to the needs and expectations of the Citizens, is to violate the Confidence of the people. Those who understand and conduct themselves as a Representative of the people know for whom they are voting. Those who believe that the votes they cast are theirs to use any way they see fit, see themselves as the Rulers of our country. No longer is their Representation about the people but about their own interests. They have lost sight of the implied expectations to be fulfilled on behalf of the people. They have redefined their job descriptions and have chosen to identify themselves with bosses other than the people who sent them to serve.

During their incumbency we are put into a position of trusting they do what's right, but if not, we are fettered against correcting our mistake until the next election cycle. We are often operating in the dark to exactly what they are doing supposedly "for us, not to us! " The lack of transparency of their actions is nothing more than a veiled attempt to prevent us from knowing the truth of their actions; things that might make us question whether our next vote on their behalf is a waste of our power and inadvertently providing a false approval of their representation.

Our vote should not be used as praise for how much they have stolen from the Treasury for their state. It should not be a reward for unethical and immoral behavior as is to often the case. They have proven time and again that they are unable to police themselves, so the time has come that we use our vote as the police force of the governed to rid the system of those who would "rule rather than represent. "

Implied Confidence

> "Public confidence in the integrity of the government is indispensable to faith in Democracy; and when we lose faith in the system, we have lost faith in everything we fight and spend for."
>
> Adlai E. Stevenson

What is our vote if not a symbol or expression "of our faith or belief that one will act in a right, proper or effective way."[3] To the people who cast their vote it is an expression of confidence in their chosen candidate. The power of a Democracy lives within the right of every American to vote for the style of government they desire. It is also the duty of the incumbent to vote the will of his constituents which is after all, the definition of Representation.

> "The only legitimate right to govern
> is an expressed grant of power "FROM" the people."
>
> President William Henry Harrison

Rep. Eric Massa stands in front of the cameras during an August 2009 interview on Health Care Reform and states that he will vote

---

3   Merriam Webster Collegiate Dictionary

the way he thinks best, regardless of the desires of his constituents. Do they really know better than their constituents the needs of the people in their states and districts? What happens to confidence when a duly elected official blatantly states that the desires and beliefs of his constituents are not important? So is he Representative or Ruler?

Sen. Christopher Dodd believes it both moral and ethical to lie to the American people about his knowledge of specifics in the Stimulus bill. Once caught, like the recalcitrant child, he tries to shift fault from himself to anyone and everyone he can think of.

Representative Pelosi accuses the CIA of always lying to congress about their activities. She and Rep. Hoyer write an op-ed accusing the people attending town hall meetings of being Nazi's or acting un-American in exercising their rights as citizens. Pelosi likening their rhetoric to approving of assassinations like those in "79 in San Francisco. Are we really un-American, is it really the right of our representative's to define us based on their own self interests? A Representative would not find exercising the right to free speech a violation of the rights of the governed; only a Ruler would interpret free speech as a violation and only when it goes against their agenda. Refresh my memory here; didn't we fight a war to defend this right? Doesn't this right to free speech appear in one or two of those pesky documents our "Founding Father" wrote, which today's politicians seem to feel are antiquated and should no longer apply as guidance to our political system?

Rep. Joe Wilson bursts out "you lie" in the Joint session of the House and Senate; he is then castigated by this leadership for his actions. They demand an apology on the floor of the House even after he apologizes to the President and his apology is accepted. But the leadership sees this as an inadequate amount of humiliation and wastes time and energy on further humiliation on the floor of the House. But shouldn't those making the demands consider apologizing for the insults they cast on all of the American people before they attempt to heap humiliation on others? What of Rep. Graysons' accusation of "people who are against healthcare reform as 'white racists," or his "if you are elderly and get sick you die," definition of Republican healthcare reform? Democrats are quick to vilify and punish Republican statements but are nowhere to be found when one of their own steps over the line. Another case in point of their lack of morals would be Sen. Reids' racist comments about then candidate Obama.

Leadership is supposed to start at the top and filter its way down but we are in a position of total incompetence disguised as leadership. If you can't respect the people you are sent to represent there is little hope that you can ever be accused of providing professional leadership or representation of the needs of your constituents.

When confidence breaks down and our representatives use the power of their vote as political capital, which is most often sold to the highest bidder, to repay their campaign debts to special interests; for the benefit of the few versus the benefit to the country as a whole. When will we take up the mantle of responsibility and become the policing force. When they trade their votes for "Pork Barrel" spending initiatives to either protect their incumbency position or those of their fellow party members, they act as Rulers not Representatives, violating the public trust. Democrat leadership purchasing the votes needed to pass healthcare reform by putting a lifetime cap on Medicaid expenses for Nebraska thereby securing NE (D) Sen. Ben Nelsons' vote; or Fl (D) Sen. Bill Nelsons' vote for the guarantee that Medicare Part D would not be discontinued in his state as it will be in the other 49 states; or LA (D) Sen. Mary Landrieu's $300 million Lousiana purchase?

If you don't live in one of these three states you're paying the freight. If you live in one of these states at least you are reimbursed a portion if not all of the freight you will pay for the other two. But for those of us in one of the other 47 states we're not even getting kissed first!

> "Here sir, the people govern; here they act by
> their immediate representatives."
> Alexander Hamilton, New York convention
> on the adoption of the Federal Constitution.

Where is the evidence of honorable and ethical behavior?

If the above statement is true, how it is that Rep. John Murtha, described appropriately as a walking, talking ethics violation, can still be in office? Under almost constant investigation for ethics violations since 1980 it would seem that the people of Pennsylvania would object to the behavior and remove him. But failing that, how is it that Ethics

Committee's fail to exercise discipline over his actions? The least they could do is give a hard yank to his curly pink tail, but it must be covered in pig grease because they just can't seem to get a good hold on it!

Unfortunately since the removal of Sen. Ted Stevens from office, a very positive move in the right direction, John Murtha has been elevated to protector of the code for the ATM of the Treasury. From the frying pan to the fire! It would seem that nobody makes a withdrawal without the prior consent of Murtha and only after he has taken what he feels is his share. With misplaced power comes unfettered violation of trust and outright fraud!

Stealing from the Treasury has become the norm rather than the exception. How as a people do we exercise the power of the vote to stop use of "OUR" Treasury as the private ATM machine of the elected officials and the special interests? How long will we put up with the idea that this abuse is just business as usual? In what world does it make sense to award 3.5 billion dollars in "PORK," as was done for Rep. Kaptur by Speaker Pelosi and Rep.Waxman for her vote on the Cap and Trade bill?

But as Sen. Reid told us on healthcare reform, "this is how the legislative process works and any Senator who didn't get his pork into this bill before passage just wasn't doing their job!" Wait a minute, is he really saying that if you don't partake in the embezzlement of the public's money you have failed your constitiuents?

Stewardship

Stewardship is defined as "the careful and responsible management of something entrusted to one's care."[4] How does this definition match up with the above definition of stewardship by Sen. Reid? Despite your faith or your lack of belief in some higher power, it would seem to me that this principal, common to most religions, would set a valuable standard of behavior that even the most atheistic among us would have a hard time arguing against.

They send millions of dollars to a town to help fight a homeless problem which the town honestly says they don't have. Hundreds of thousands of dollars sent to a university to study the effects of listening

---

4   Merriam Webster Collegiate Dictionary

on performance? Some 30 thousand dollars for storytellers and basket weavers? Finally basket weaving 101 is recognized as a career! They borrow 2 billion dollars from China and turn around and give it back to them in the form of a grant for study of green technologies?

September 2009 the law banning firearms in checked baggage on Amtrak, put into effect after 9/11, is repealed, now making it legal. To facilitate the change they award 1.6 billion dollars to Amtrak! My question is what is there to start up? Are they using the money to provide everyone a firearm before boarding?

New Amtrak Ad
For a limited time only
Ride Amtrak today and receive your FREE personalized 357!
(Ammo not included.)

With some 10,000 pork projects funded through the 2008/2009 federal budget and over 100 in the Stimulus bill, examples of poor Stewardship are actually quite endless. Does this instill your confidence? Why are we reluctant to use the power of the vote to remove those incapable of stewardship, representatives who find it expedient to vote their will rather than the will of their constituents or those who create the lack of confidence through their lack of morals, honesty and integrity? As a nation have we collectively lost our interest in society and can now only focus on what's in it for me? Does it take a PHD to figure out why the majority of Defense Contractors maintain an office, some of them no more than an address with no real staff or production, in Murtha's District?

"We believe above all else
that those who hold in their hands the power of government
must themselves be independent-
and this kind of independence means the wisdom,
the experience, the courage to identify the special interests
and the pressures that are always at work,
to see the public interest steadily,
to resist its subordination no matter the political hazards"
Adlai E. Stevenson

It's that pesky last statement that always seems to trip them up. They just don't seem able to clear that bar!

Have you ever wondered why the citizens of the United States are never able to achieve "Special Interest" status? Shouldn't the American people be not just the largest special interest but the "Only" special interest?

Is it time that we look at term limits as the only way that we have of protecting our assets? Looking at the behavior of many of our politicians doesn't it seem as though the message they are sending us is how important the concept of term limits is to our future stability as a country and society? It is obvious the Constitution never intended that "opportunity to serve" would inevitably become a profession, so has the time come that 20, 30 or 40 years be no longer acceptable? We have term limits on mayors, county governments and state governorships even the position of President of The United States, but none on serving in Congress! Why is that?

Our goal should be that we find and elect citizens who will stay faithful to the confidence of the American people rather than the madness of making decisions based on the protection of their own incumbency? At the first whiff of abuse of power, decisions that line their pockets with no positive affect for the citizen, abuse of campaign finance laws and the blatant demonstration that they know better than we what is good for the country as a whole, we must be prepared to exercise the power of our vote and reestablish lost Confidence.

Their focus should be always on the good of the Republic and when their aim falters our aim should be to replace them. Give them the freedom to pursue their own interest's full time, outside of the government, which is where greed, self enrichment and self aggrandizement belong and where the shareholders have the legal power to deal with it. Political service, contrary to popular belief of many who serve, is not supposed to be the avenue to create personal wealth, but rather to protect the rights of every citizen to build theirs. Lets start treating this as just what it is; the largest Corporation in the world and we the shareholders!

The essence of Government is power; and power,
lodged as it must be in human hands, will ever be liable to abuse.
James Madison

I would submit that conventions behind closed doors for the purpose of making decisions without the transparency of light behind them, the habit of loosening laws of process to make it easier for them to pass their hidden agenda's and the failure of ethics committee's to properly police their colleagues regarding abuse of power, must be halted, changed and made unacceptable. After all, isn't that the very behavior of corporations which has our members of Congress all a twitter?

Like any other investment you need to always assess its return to you. The rest of this book is about looking at the return we receive for the investment of our vote.

Chapter 2

"The Day the Well Ran Dry!"

On April 25, 2009 our budget went from all cash to all credit for Fiscal Year 2008/2009. We are approaching five hundred billion dollars a year in interest charges on a debt approaching 13 trillion dollars. Does it excite and mistify you when David Copperfield makes a 747 or the Statue of Liberty disappear? Then you have got to love the magic being performed everyday within the Halls of Congress!

As we already discussed, a government of Representatives are expected to exercise stewardship over the assets and resources of the governed. This lack of stewardship answers the question of "Representatives or Rulers." They used to be called Kings, Queens and Czars, the ruling class. When they overspent their treasuries they simply went back to the people they ruled, increased taxes, seized assets and replenished their treasuries on the backs of the ruled. They obviously have new titles today but there shenanigans remain the same. They bleed us and bleed us with the ultimate goal being that we are too busy today trying to survive to be able to keep up with everything they do to keep us down. "Eyes always looking down will never see where they are going!"

This year we made it to April; in 2010 will we make it past March? At the current pace of spending my calculations indicate that by 2015 we will witness for the first time in history all revenues for fiscal year 2015/2016 will be spent prior to September 2015. In other words our expenditures will outpace our revenues by a full 13 months! So I ask you; do we have reason to be fearful if we bring our eyes up so we can see the destination?

We bought it hook line and sinker during the 2008 elections. Did it seem to you as though every candidate from President on down was running on a platform of no more business as usual? The culture of Washington D.C., corruption, self interest and raiding of the treasury for personal interests were done! Finally the ERA of transparency had arrived! Washington insiders were now going to be the Washington outsiders.

Chapter 3

Billed as a "New Era of Responsibility," they even wrote a book with the same title!

Let's take a look at the "President's Message from the Blue Collar Perspective of the many ills we suffer and the cures proposed along with how we have progressed toward these goals thus far. We can't expect overnight solutions or results but we should be able to find evidence that we have found the right road.

We are where we are because of "...an era of profound irresponsibility that engulfed both private and public institutions from some of our largest companies' executive suites to the seats of power in Washington D.C." "...a lack of transparency created a situation in which serious economic dangers were visible to all too few."[5]

The cures as laid out in this "New Era of Responsibility" will shine under the golden glare of the midday sun, except for TARP, STIMULUS, HEALTHCARE and CAP AND TRADE. These are just too important to let you in on their construction.

"...For decades, too many on Wall Street threw caution to the wind, chased profits with blind optimism and little regard for serious risk—and with even less regard for the public good." But aren't these the same behaviors we see daily within the halls of Congress? For decades Congress has created departments, organizations and entitlement programs without any thought given to how these programs would be funded. How many years has Washington D.C. been warning us that Medicare, Medicaid and Social Security were basically insolvent? And

---

5   A New Era of Responsibility – Renewing America's Promise - President's Message

now they want to Nationalize Healthcare at trillions of dollars and "just trust them" has become the new mantra. "...once we pass it and put it into practice people are going to love it," President Obama during the week of January 13th. Maybe, but what is it exactly, how much will it really cost and where will the money come from to fund it?

"Lenders made loans without concern for whether borrowers could repay them. Inadequately informed of the risks and overwhelmed by the fine print, many borrowers took on debt they could not really afford." Do these accusations sound to you like the same behavior's which created the Stimulus package which now has the taxpayers exposed to an estimated $23 Trillion Dollars of government guarantees? You would have thought that we would have learned our lesson with Fannie Mae and Freddie Mac, A.I.G., Citibank and to automakers?

Now they are entrenched in the creation of yet another "Jobs Stimulus" bill spending somewhere between $80 and $150 billion. How will they pay for it? The way Congress always pays for bills; they are going to use the repayments from businesses bailed out by the TARP bill! The billed specified that when the funds started to be repaid they would have to go to deficit reduction, but Congress if nothing else is consistent. They will simply pass another bill or amendment that allows them to redirect the funds from deficit reduction to their new "Job Stimulus" bill.

We all should have learned by now that our government has never met a debt that they weren't willing to delay repaying. How else can you explain how we currently have a $14 Trillion deficit?

It goes on to say that "...they forgot that markets work best when there is transparency and accountability and when the rules of the road are both fair and vigorously enforced. For years, a lack of transparency created a situation in which serious economic dangers were visible to all too few." Transparency, to shed light on, was the campaign mantra for all of 2007 and 2008. Now we hear about all of the mistakes in the bailouts with retention bonuses, performance bonuses, corporate retreats etc, etc. Interestingly enough, as you will see in this book, Congress has a proclivity for the same behaviors. Then we have untold billions of dollars put into Fannie Mae and Freddie Mac which they now want to close down. Wouldn't it have made more sense to close them before the flushing of the taxpayer's money?

"…we cannot depend on government alone to create jobs or to generate long term growth. Ours is a market economy…" But government has been the only source thus far for job creation, by some 30%. For example, the Social Security Dept. just spent $30 million in an effort to hire 585 new employees! That is $52,282 per new hire which would make the Blue Collar Person pause and think maybe it is time to review the hiring process.

"This plan's provisions will put money in the pockets of the American people, save or create at least(!) (my emphasis) three and a half million jobs, and help to revive our economy. The people I know and talk to have had money put into their pocket, including myself, thanks to the unemployment benefit extensions and the government contributions for Cobra benefits on health insurance. But is this the money they are talking about? If not we are currently looking at 26 million people with empty pockets.

"…the Recovery Act and the (2009/2010) budget will make long overdue investments in priorities-like clean energy, education, healthcare and a new infrastructure – that are necessary to keep us strong and competitive in the 21st Century." So we are putting $1.5 billion into FutureGen, the clean burning coal plant utilizing Carbon Monoxide sequestration technology in Chicago. Meanwhile ignoring studies that show the technology, design and purposes for the plant are already obsolete and the amount earmarked is little more than half of the total cost. Ask yourself; where will they come up with the balance of the money needed to complete the plant?

Teachers are being laid off across the country while stimulus dollars are spent on new equipment and other expenditures that don't improve the quality of education. It would seem that teachers are rapidly becoming redundant when you take into consideration that we are laying them off and instead investing in technology to prepare our kids for the future. I guess the new computers will teach the kids. And then you have school districts like some in New York where there are hundreds of teachers not allowed to teach, while drawing a full salary, and awaiting disciplinary action, some waiting for years, for some infraction they committed. With the hundreds of thousands of dollars being spent, $750,000 in New York alone, couldn't they speed up the review process and either fire these teachers or clear them and get them back into the classroom? No, it makes more sense for them to report each day to the disciplinary storage room where they sit and read or watch movies day in and day out. This makes as much sense as automakers having to continue to pay employees that have been laid off for lack of work. Who in their right mind could ever think that this makes good sense? While you are thanking the unions for this indefensible idea remember, these are the same unions who just received special tax exemptions for their Cadillac healthcare plans. And you thought the days for successful lobbying were over!

All that new infrastructure like the Ecopassage in Florida to save the lives of thousand of turtles that seek the murkier swamps on the other side of the freeway. It will only cost us about $10 million to build the passage way. That much money, if my math is correct, would pay $50,000 per year for the next 200 years to herd the turtles across the highway.

What about all of the bridge's being refitted with the newest earthquake technology even though they only service 20 or 30 cars a day. That's right; these are some of the infrastructure investments our money is going for. But alas, not the only ones, many more follow later in this book. Projects like the bridge Florida wants to build a quarter mile from an existing bridge to the same destination. The Stimulus money is being used to buy the land but won't buy more than half. And there is no guarantee that the owners even want to sell the land.

"...fundamentally reform our healthcare system, delivering quality care to more Americans while reducing costs for us all." "...not only change what Washington invests in but how Washington does business. "...a lack of transparency created a situation in which serious economic dangers were visible to all too few."[6]

So let's not let the citizens know exactly what our healthcare reform methods are. We just move the committee behind closed doors and put together whatever we can and pass it. All people need to know is that they will love whatever we come up with. After all didn't Steny Hoyer say "it's better than nothing?" This will go a long way to '...rebuilding that lost trust and confidence." What do you mean how are we going to pay for it? It will not only be budget neutral but will actually reduce

---

6   A New Era of Responsibility – Renewing America's Promise - President's Message

the deficit over the next ten years! What do you mean you want to know how? We've told you time and again "just trust us we've got it covered!"

"…while our Budget will run deficits, we must begin the process of making the tough choices necessary to restore fiscal discipline, cut the deficit in half by the end of my first term in office, and put our Nation on sound fiscal footing." And we are going to do just that as soon as we add $1.5 trillion dollars to the deficit for 2009/2010 and another $1.3 Trillion for the 2010/2011 budget. Yes these are big gaps but never fear, we are putting a spending freeze into effect starting in 2011 that will save $25 Billion in government operating costs per year. If you, like I, were worried about these deficits we can all now take a deep breath and say "okay I guess they do have it covered!"

"We should never forget that our workers are more innovative and industrious than any on earth." Okay so what you are really saying is that we just have to find them jobs and we're good to go? Well why didn't you say so before? After all that is what the Stimulus Bill is doing right? I guess it's a perception problem. What you forgot to tell us is most of these "innovative and industrious workers" are already back to work in those invisible districts reporting jobs saved. Well shoot, there for a minute I thought we were in trouble. Thanks for clearing that up! And to think, we were losing "trust and confidence."

"We can restore opportunity and prosperity. And we can bring about a new sense of responsibility among Americans from every walk of life and from every corner of America." How will we do it? It's simple really. We are going to start taxing the rich in America and distribute it to those who have less. There you go, that takes care of the prosperity problem now we just have to resolve the opportunity issue. We're half way there and its only been a year.

Well great! I can think of 26 million Americans that are ready for that to happen so why don't you go ahead and get started on that today. What do you mean you can't do it if you have to do it on C-Span? Are you telling us that you misspoke dozens of times during your campaign? Okay, now I get it! You are counting every C-Span broadcast of government in action (?) as fulfilling this campaign promise.[7] Or, maybe it is just a case of these broadcasts you are counting are airing

---

7   Speech to Republican retreat Jan. 29, 2010

only in those mythical congressional districts where they created and saved all those jobs you keep bragging about.

The practice of "Pork Barrel Spending" was finally going to be moved from "behind the closed doors horse trading of the past into the light of day for all to see." No more would the special interests be given their Debit Card to draw away our resources. No more would the lobbyists write the bills voted on by our duly elected representatives. Finally they would resume the practice of writing their own bills and all would find the time to read the bills before they voted. Transparency in everything they do.

"We will go through the budget line by line to root out the abuse, waste and fraud of the National Treasury."[8] My understanding from this statement is that this was to start January 20, 2009. We are now in the end of January 2010 and the time and commitment to this campaign promise has yet to be found.

The size of government has increased some 30%. We have approximately 32 Czars appointed requiring no vetting process by the Senate and no disclosure of how much these people are being paid. Our elected officials managed to insert over 10,000 "pork Barrel Spending" bills into the 2008/2009 budget. The Presidents Stimulus Bill included over 100 sides of PORK. We were officially broke by April 25, 2009. The leaders of the House paid 3.5 billion dollars for a single vote on their Cap and Trade Bill. It's hard to find even the notion that this is a "New Era of Responsibility."

Though the members of Congress are now required to post their "Pork" on their websites it didn't come without a fight and most still do not post them in a manner that makes it easy to identify them. They still don't post their office operating expenditures online where they can be audited by the citizens. Though corporations have been brought to task by the "holier than thou" attitude of the House Finance Committee, for corporate retreats, huge bonuses and misuse of Corporate Jets, it turns out that these very same members of Congress exercise the same abuse, the only difference being that they are using taxpayer money not shareholder money.

It seems like their own behavior is always seen through rose colored glasses. In their eyes the questions of morals and ethics never seem to

---

8   Campaign promise by then Sen. Barack Obama

be the issue, but I would say that it is exactly the issue since it is this behavior that got us to where we are today. If morals, ethics and honesty are not apparent in those who govern on our behalf it is unreasonable to think that they are capable of being the watchdog over those same qualities in those they govern.

This "New Era" seems as though it cries out for us to take into our own hands the legislating of morals, ethics and honesty through the power of the vote. It is time to demonstrate to them that the votes they cast do not belong to them to be cast in a manner as to increase their power or personal interests. These votes belong to the people and are to be used to make the plight of the people better! If they continue to abuse this privilege then it is our absolute responsibility to replace them with someone who does.

The mantra of the "New Era" is "just trust us, we can fix these problems." Trust is no longer a privilege we should bestow upon them given their performance thus far. If you want trust you need to earn it and not reading a bill before you vote, insertion of over 10,000 pork projects into a budget, claiming jobs saved when you know there is no way to measure, all seem to me actions that won't instill trust but rather raise the red flags of doubt and distrust that should become the focus of the next election cycle.

In any corporation the budgeting process is one of careful line by line consideration and revenue is projected on logical predictions of the market place. If your revenue projections come up short you will find yourself in deficit spending and adjustments will need to be made quickly. Unfortunately our government lacks the ability to react quickly and all to often lack's the ability to forecast on logical predictions of revenue and expenses. That is how we end up with estimated revenue increasing even though we are in the biggest recession in the last 60 years.

The Congressional Budget Office is a non partisan branch of the government under the control of Congress not the Administration, its purpose to calculate the costs in any given bill by predicting current and future expenditures as well as realistic revenue estimations. According to their estimate we now sit on an exposure of 23 Trillion Dollars *($76,666 for each of the 300 million citizens)* resulting from the expenditures of money and government loan guarantees which were made with the implementation of this the Stimulus bill. In all fairness the numbers assume the worst case scenario; but what if?

Make no mistake about it; the United States is the largest corporation on earth and we are doomed if we cannot make an honest assessment of revenue and expenditures. If we are not willing to go after the waste, corruption and outright thievery prevalent under the current system how is their a realistic hope of surviving as a country?

They say the definition of insanity is doing the same thing over and over again but expecting different results. Perhaps the only way it will ever come about is if we take seriously the power of our vote and we start using it to remove the morally and ethically challenged, those who would steal our money for payment of their own political debts and put people in office who are willing to put the *"good of the American People"* before their self interests.

Our hope's and dreams were that you were the politician who would quit giving us broken promises and what if's. Instead we have received irresponsibly increased spending, no change in governments lack of transparency and results that are not easily proven if they can be proven at all. Shifting definitions of the promises you made and the results you told us to expect can only lead us to believe that you cannot live up to them.

Chapter 4

Cure Worse Than Disease?

Information, pros and cons, fly through the media and the Congress faster than a rocket leaving earth's atmosphere. What it says or doesn't say seems to depend on what day of the week it is. Illegal immigrants covered or not, abortion paid for with taxpayer money or not and where will all the money come from. Will there be healthcare czars who make the determination of the value of your receiving emergency medical attention? Will the system be directed by a federal budget that says, "when the money is gone the treatments stop?" Does the government really have the power to mandate that all citizens buy insurance or be fined? How many new people can and will be enrolled? Does it lead to rationing?

In spite of claims to the contrary by the President, this legislation has been anything but transparent as evidenced by his very own words; "…if the bill becomes law the American people will suddenly learn that this bill does things they like." If creation of the bill had truly been transparent, as the administration would like us to believe, why would we suddenly learn things we like? It seems to me that if there was transparency as they claim, we should already know what was in the bill and therefore wouldn't be surprise. He has also said that "…I haven't done a good enough job of explaining this bill to the people."

To me this infers that we are too dense to understand his explanations in the 29 speeches he has already given on this bill. I would proffer the explanation that if we don't understand it at this point it isn't a problem of not being able to understand his speeches but rather, that he and the Democrats themselves don't understand what is in the bill.

So many questions and so few answers but once again time is of the essence. If this reform is to be passed where will it really take us? Will we end up in the same place that the TARP and Stimulus bills took us? Who do we believe; Democrats, Republicans, Independents or none of them? Can we trust any of them? Again we see the American people saying no but our Representatives don't want to listen.

This Administration seems to operate with the same Bush doctrine; if you're not with us you are against us. The difference being Bush was referring to our allied nations which joined us in the war against terror. President Obama believes the Citizens of this country who question are the ones against him. To question is to criticize and this Administration doesn't accept criticism well at all. Their battle lines aren't drawn in the sand but in cement.

The following is an independent review of what the bill really says and what it will mean to the Blue Collar American.[9]

Perhaps the best indicator of where this legislation is taking us is the I.R.S. tax code. Envision if you will, how many thousands of pages of regulations will need to be written for a legislative bill that will, in its final form, be some 2000 to 3000 pages long. With the creation of over 100 new bureaucratic institutions, each with its own powers of enforcement, imagine the paperwork and bureaucracy we will have to wade through for the most routine of treatments. Does this feel like your medical decisions will be between you and your doctor exclusively? Do you really believe that with the creation of this much bureaucracy we can expect less paperwork to make our system function or that privacy will be attainable? Show me a government department that has ever decreased and not increased the volume of paperwork.

In case you plan to keep your private insurance plan the odds are not in your favor that what you have now, although they keep saying you can keep it, very likely won't exist in this new system. This bill puts government right in the middle of operations of insurance companies. In fact they could be considered the C.E.O of every company because through this bill they will dictate the specifics of each plan offered, they will have the authority to dictate accounting methods, premiums, claims payouts, profits and losses as well as what constitutes government approved coverage.

With a new commission called "Health Choices Commissioner"

---

9   http://docs.house.gov/rules/health/111_ahcaa.pdf

responsible for overseeing the new healthcare system it is unlikely that we will be able to prevent the overtaking of our system by the government. You might also ask why, if choices are going to be left between your doctor and yourself, why we need a Health "Choices" Commissioner. Can we expect to retain our individual rights when the bill is written to allow the total takeover of our healthcare system? Once this door is opened there is little likelihood that we will ever be able to close it again.

Can't afford to carry insurance? Then be ready to be taxed in order to make amends for your poverty or because you are young and healthy. What happens if you don't carry the proper coverage, at any time during the year, as determined by your government? You will be taxed. Or maybe your coverage adjusts during the year and falls below the threshold. Then be ready to pay a tax of 2.5% of your modified gross income.

But just to make it even more fun for the taxpayer the "Health Choices Commissioner" can change the definition of coverage minimums at any time during the year, which means we can be taxed for falling below these minimum standards.

You can expect that many insurance carriers will likely go out of business because they can no longer meet the requirements enforced by the government. Catastrophic insurance carried by many people to cover any hospitalization or medical catastrophe will not qualify under the governments requirements and therefore will add additional costs to this group of people. Their option is to enroll in the government plan or pay taxes for their nonconformity.

Creation of a "Health Benefits Advisory Committee" is for the purposes of controlling the public and private plans." This means that the federal government will now determine the specifics of the policies allowed to be sold by the insurance carriers. But wait you say; wasn't one of the big results of this bill supposed to be the introduction of more competition in the marketplace? Its hidden agenda is to drive people into the government plan further reducing the public insurance options. This committee will serve other functions such as the use of actuarial numbers to drive costs down for Medicare and Medicaid.

This means that your treatment will be measured against people with similar medical problems and will determine if you are receiving too little or too much treatment. It will be used as a tool for reducing payments for reoccurrence or readmission to the hospital more than once for the same illness. This committee then holds power over doctor and hospital payments which will directly affect the healthcare of all. They will define the definition of excessive treatment and, to a large extent, the profitability of doctors and hospitals that serve Medicare and Medicaid patients. Control of levels of treatment and or multiple hospitalizations will help to bring statistics down which then becomes a vicious cycle of reducing costs through declining treatment. And remember that they intend to increase the membership in both of these government plans. Sounds, smells and feels like rationing of medical care to me. How about you?

Logically if we have rationing we cannot help but start to create waiting lists and the legislation passed thus far speaks directly to that expectation by excluding children from the waiting list. There are also reporting standards requiring disclosure of the extent of and who is on the waiting list for treatment.

If you have had the good fortune to be financially successful in your life, I think they call it living the dream, would you be so good as to pick up a portion of the healthcare for those who haven't been as successful? You see you simply have too much and we too little so the only fair thing is for you to pay for them. Sounds, smells and feels like redistribution of wealth to me. How about you?

But wait! Many of you have found your piece of the dream by growing your own business, so here is one way you can get some of your money back. If your medical insurance coverage is too hard on your bottom line, or you would just like to get out of providing insurance here is what you do. Simply cancel your insurance and your employees will have to go onto the government plan. Sure there is an 8% penalty to your company but what the heck; it's cheaper than paying for the coverage you have been providing. Presto! You just recouped part of your wealth tax back thanks to the short foresight of our government officials. And you helped move the government one step closer to its goal of total takeover.

The real effect of this legislation will be to increase the roles which in turn will increase the expenses of treatment which will in turn increase the level of the waiting lists and result in increased rationing.

But the government is willing to pay this price because they have already exempted federal workers and members of Congress from this reform. That is right; everything stays the same for them as it is now! What a country huh!

Representatives would be our equals. Rulers are our betters and by continually excluding themselves from what they subject us to they are saying they really see themselves as Rulers!

Businesses will see increased paperwork and record keeping to meet reporting requirements. Individuals and businesses will be subject to audits and the government will decide the extent of any records that be provided. Will this grow to include our medical records? Only the commissioners and committee's will make that eventual decision; but what does history show when government is trying to control its citizens?

So just how does the government plan to pay for all of this coverage? Thus far it is the Super Bowl of semantics. Not with new taxes of course; unless you own rental properties, receive stock dividends or capital gains. If you have a Cadillac insurance plan and don't belong to the unions, because Obama exempted them from the tax as a payback for election support, you will be paying as much as 40% excise tax. But they claim it isn't a tax but a fee, which seems rather odd since it says tax right in the name. Kind of like all of the new jobs reported where stimulus money was used; excise tax is really a fee and a pay increase is a new job!

What do you do if you require any type of medical device? The medical equipment manufacturer's decided not to play ball with the White House so the bill now includes a 40% tax on all medical equipment. I don't have a PHD in economics but it isn't to hard to figure out that, while the White House would like us to believe the companies will absorb this tax as a cost of doing business, I am pretty sure that they will be tacking it onto the price of their equipment. It is as if the administration really believes their semantics. Poor, middle class and rich alike, if you need the equipment you will be paying the tax!

It is just the cost of not playing ball with this administration. The lobbyists for the industry chose not to offer their public support for the healthcare reform bill and within days found themselves looking at a new tax. Rather than costing to play the game this case is about the cost of not playing the game. Taxation runs amuck!

Say you are an insulin dependant diabetic and your doctor decides you need an insulin pump. This pump decreases the amount of insulin you require plus it provides much better blood sugar control. This device cost approximately $7,000 to purchase of which your insurance carrier pays about $6,000. There is equipment that needs to be used in conjunction with the pump which needs to be changed every 3 days. The cost of this replaceable equipment is may be as much as $1,000 per month.

The 40% tax on the pump itself would increase the price to about $10,500 and the monthly cost of the replaceable equipment would run about $1,400 per month. Will the insurance, whether government or private, be likely to cover the higher cost? What about Medicare? With the largest segment of the population, with diabetes, being the elderly, it seems logical that they will have to raise their premiums if they are going to cover the increased costs. So is this a tax increase on the middle class? Not by their definition but it equates to the same thing because you'll have to pay the increased cost to retain your current coverage and they have already stated that they are looking at increasing our Medicare payroll taxes to cover the growth of the population that will be enrolled on Medicare. So, the Administration taxes the manufacturer but doesn't have to call it a tax on the middle class or any other class in the country because we don't directly pay the increase. It's all a game of semantics and flies in the face of truth or transparency. They just can't admit to what they are doing.

In the great healthcare reform sellout you can be sure that the middle class, whom he guaranteed would not pay any new taxes, will not make it through unscathed. Have a Cadillac plan but don't belong to a union? There is a tax for that? Do you require medical equipment? There is a tax for that? Are you young and in good health so don't have a need for insurance? There is a tax for that? Do you own a company that doesn't offer employee medical plans? There is a tax for that? Can't afford the cost of insurance? There is a tax for that? Can't afford to carry minimum coverage as defined by the Health Choice Commissioner? There is a tax for that? Have to buy prescriptions every month? There is a tax for that? Chalk this one up to the drug manufacturer sellout by the administration.

With this takeover we will see a tremendous growth in the rolls of Medicaid and with this growth seriously increasing costs. These costs will be born by the individual states which are currently struggling to fill huge gaps in their budgets. So where will the funds come from to cover these new Medicaid costs? I probably don't need to say it but, from you and I obviously. The benefit to the administration for the shifting of these costs is that it enables them to still claim no new taxes to the middle class. But who are you and I?

We do have one avenue open to us to avoid these new taxes imposed by our states; we all simply move to Nebraska where the biggest winner in Healthcare Reform great giveaway got his State exempted into perpetuity by transferring their increased Medicaid costs back to the Federal Government.

And the winner is…

Sen. Ben Nelson (D) NE having said recently "…my vote is not for sale" evidently meant for a set price. Now give me an incalculable number that will carry into perpetuity and you've got yourself a vote!

It's important to point out here that the Constituents of Nebraska deserve recognition for their immediate negative response to the behavior of their Senator.

Rep. Mary Landrieu (D) LA assures everyone that "…I can't be bought" evidently meant that while she can't be bought she certainly doesn't shy away from bribery. To the tune of $300 million her vote was cast lock stock and barrel for healthcare reform.

Michigan buys a pass for Michigan Blue Cross insurance plan tax.

Florida, Pennsylvania and New York receive exempt status allowing them to keep Medicare Plan D while the other 47 States will see tax increases to offset the cost of these exemptions.

And the loser is…

The rest of us who don't reside in one of the "Special" states. We will receive none of these benefits but will get to pay higher taxes to cover these expenditures.

This is starting to sound like an iPhone commercial. For everything you do, regardless of your class, unless you are a Federal worker, resident of one of the "Special" states or a member of Congress, there is an app. (read tax), for that.

As I write this book, February 3, 2010 it is uncertain whether Congress will be able to force this bill upon us or not, but the one thing that is for sure is that they are not interested or concerned for the citizens of this country. It is this very apathy which provides the largest danger to our country. We are allowing our Constitution to be turned into a fictional document because we the citizens continue to allow our Representatives Ruler status.

There are a never ending list of problems and questions with this legislation and illegal immigrants are like a huge black hole for me; a question of morality, compassion and common sense. On the one hand we don't want to reward illegal behavior but at the same time we are a compassionate nation. Then if you take the common sense approach, which very well means we are ignoring our other feelings, we already pay for these people to receive medical treatment.

Our compassionate nature has caused us to pass laws that prevent hospitals from providing medical treatment based on financial means. For the same reason that our citizens who cannot afford medical insurance use our emergency rooms for the medical care provider so too do illegal immigrants.

So now does it make sense to over look the illegal aspect of their presence and include them in healthcare reform? Or do we cut off our nose to spite our face by denying them participation? If we allow them coverage will they even sign up? And if they don't do we continue to say our medical system has to turn them away?

I admit I don't know the answer. Like so many my knee jerk reaction is to turn them away but how do I accept the compromise of my compassion, my belief in the law or the human aspect that requires punishment?

Chapter 5

Do As I Say, Not As I Do!

Sound familiar? If you were raised like me, then you probably heard that from one or both of your parents. If you like me are a parent, you have probably said it to your kids. It is usually used in a situation where you are asking for behavior different from your own. Why? Most likely because your behavior is less than appropriate and you really can't defend it. But is this acceptable behavior from our Politicians?

I don't think, for the most part, our elected officials are stupid. But you have to think their belief is that we are. How else can you possibly explain the self righteous, holier than thou show they put on for all of us? Would we not have to be pretty gullible if we were to fall for their self righteous indignation?

If you need a demonstration of how disconnected our politicians are with the intelligence and perception of the Blue Collar worker watch the testimony of Edward Liddy CEO of AIG before the House Financial Services Subcommittee on March 19, 2009. See if you don't feel the embarrassment that I felt. Who among us wouldn't have gotten up, told these politicians where they could put their double talk and hypocrisy and walked out? I know I would have?

Here is a man who responded to Treasury Secretary Paulson's request to come out of retirement to help save AIG from total collapse. With an extensive background in the Insurance industry he was the most qualified person to ask to step in. He answered that call and also agreed to perform the job at $1.00 per year.

Less than 6 months later he is grilled by this subcommittee over the failures of management in AIG prior to his joining the company.[10] He was blamed for everything from retention pay contracts, which were in place prior to his taking over, to having caused the collapse. At one point when he expressed his perception of being insulted and his good name brought into question MA. Senator Lynch (D) questioning him at the time actually stated that he was glad it was perceived that way because that is exactly how he intended to be perceived. Beyond rude and arrogant this Senator should have been severely reprimanded for his lack of civility and at the least he owes a serious apology to Mr. Liddy for his lack of manners. Additionally he should perhaps take a closer look at the behaviors of the august body he belongs too before criticizing someone who answered his governments call.

Note: It was later revealed that these same politicians were aware of the retention contracts in the TARP bill. See the Chapter on "Politician Turned Recalcitrant Child."

It can only be described as the perfect example of "do as I say, not as I do." To illustrate this point look at how they conduct business within their own offices and example expenditures for operation of said office. As you read it keep in mind their accusations and criticism.

They are each a small company themselves.

Each member of the House and Senate receives an annual operating allowance of between 1.3 million and 4.5 million dollars[11] which is intended to be spent on salaries, office operating expenses, equipment as well as travel. Granted they try to hide the way they spend these budgets as well as their other behaviors every bit as questionable as any corporation they now want to micromanage.

Retention Bonuses

And what about the issue of bonuses? It turns out that it is and has been a pretty common practice among legislators. Brendan Daly, spokesperson for Nancy Pelosi says she uses the bonus idea, as "a small perk for underpaid government employees."

---

10   To View testimony go to video.nytimes.com/video/2009/03/18/ business/1194838727568/a-i-g-chief-testifies-on-bonuses.html

11   Wall Street Journal June 2, 2009 "Lawmakers Keep Expenses Offline"

Financial Services Committee Chairman Barney Frank in 2008 awarded bonuses to dozens of staffers because "government workers are pretty low paid" according to Spokesman Steven Adamske.

Bonuses paid out to 89 staffers totaled over $300,000 or approximately $3,300 each were paid out by politicians who lost their re-election bids. Thelma Drake who lost her Virginia seat says that the $40,000 paid out to about a dozen aids were "a form of severance pay to staffers who worked their hearts out and who were now losing their jobs." How many of us have lost our jobs but not received a bonus?

Retiring lawmakers awarded approximately $283,000 in bonuses at the end of 2008. Heather Wilson of New Mexico stated that it had been "her practice for over 10 years to give bonuses at the end of the year." Spokesman for Rep. Loretta Sanchez Adrienne Elrod states that his boss is proud of the bonuses she is able to give." I ask you, who wouldn't love to give other peoples money away as bonuses?

Here let me get the check on this one!

This article came out in the Wall Street Journal June 26, 2009 (the link is below) and it is titled;

"Loan-Repayment Benefit Grows for Hill Staffers."

[12] A little known benefit of being a "non-elected staff member, lawyers, FBI agents and intelligence officials," in fiscal year 2007 had received approximately $42 Million for repayment of their college bills and student loans. For 2009 it will reach an estimated $60 Million according to government officials and records. In 2002 there were an estimated "690 employees in the executive branch which received a total of $3 Million, but by 2007 this number had risen to an estimated 6600 recipients of $42 Million."

They are using taxpayer dollars to payback loans made from taxpayer dollars to the benefit of their employees and make themselves look like heroes in the process. It's always easy to look heroic with other people's money. Again this is different because they are using taxpayer dollars not shareholder dollars!

---

12 Congress calls it "recruitment or retention incentive" http://online.wsj.com/article/SB124578152192043001.html#printMode

But as tax payers we net out under this program with a direct loss of the original loan amount plus any interest these loans would have returned. Oh yeah, don't forget that we are borrowing this money raising our deficit and paying interest on the money so that we can pay ourselves back on a loan that we were supposed to make interest on!

Interestingly enough they have a very specific name for this program; "Recruitment and Retention Incentives." Refresh my memory; where have we heard that phrase before?

But it doesn't stop there!

In addition these staffers are also entitled to participate in "education related perks" supposedly to improve their value as government employees. With another $3 Million plus they can partake in courses during work hours in such valuable subjects as Pilates, yoga, something called "The Senate's Vice Presidential Bust Collection, Home buying for Beginners, How to use a Blackberry, and Capital Building History."

Look you've done such a great job I just feel I have to...

My personal favorite, Rep. Tom Udall leaves the house to run for the New Mexico Senate seat. Several staff members took leaves of absence to work for his campaign. When he returned to Washington after winning the race he had accrued a large surplus in his budget, because he wasn't in Washington doing his job, and decided to use it to increase the salaries for 19 of his 22 employees who took the leave of absence to work in his campaign. Don't you just love it!?

In other words he used his budget funds to compensate the campaign workers, which sounds suspiciously like Wall Street, raising their annualized compensation to $163,795. Compare this amount to the approximate $170,000 paid to Senators and it makes you wonder why they are making 95% of what the boss makes. So just what are campaign funds supposed to be used for?

Lets go somewhere and talk.

Amidst all of the outrage over AIG and other TARP fund recipients over company retreats and other corporate outings "Senate records for the office of Majority Leader Harry Reid includes a $23,650 item marked "Per Diem Expenses for Staff Retreat Held in Annapolis

MD."[13] Jim Manley, a spokesman for Mr. Reid's office states that "such retreats are common practice in Congress and Industry." Wait a minute; did they forget the accusations made against corporations for the very same practice? Oh that's right, it's different when your just spending the taxpayer money. I keep forgetting about that distinction.

Flights of Entitlement

Speaker of the House Nancy Pelosi returns home to San Francisco virtually every weekend and sometimes 2 or 3 times a week. You're probably thinking the same thing I am; I'd hate to have her travel bill! Well I'm sorry to tell you this but you and I both are paying that bill. By Air Force provided jets she meanders back and forth across country. What does it cost you might ask? Well here's the thing; because we aren't shareholders, just taxpayers, we don't meet the bar of "need to know."

In the world of corporate jet usage detailed records are kept according to I.R.S. laws. If usage by any individual within or outside of the corporation is deemed to be of personal or non-corporate business the real time operating costs associated with that usage is added to that individual's tax return as taxable income. Since so many of them, some even sitting in judgment over the I.R.S., can't seem to get their tax returns right what do you suppose the odds are that they would include an expense like this on their tax return? Does anybody know; does TurboTax have a category for private jet travel?

Couldn't they at least lease American? After all we do own the companies!

For the year 2008 Florida Rep. Alcee Hastings spent $24,730 in taxpayer money to lease a 2008 luxury Lexus hybrid sedan. Louisiana Rep. Rodney Alexander paid $20,000 for a 2009 lease on a Toyota Highlander. Appropriate he says "because he comes from the largest

---

13   Online.wsj.com/article/SB124381530535870685.html "Lawmakers have long rewarded their aides with Bonuses
*Note June 5, 2009 House Speaker Nancy Pelosi goes public with recommendation that operating budgets be put online in an effort at transparency

district in his home state." Makes you wonder what the politicians from Texas must be driving, doesn't it?[14]

Approximately 130 of the 435 House lawmakers spent a combined $82,000 each month on auto leases for their offices during 2007 according to, Taxpayers for Common Sense.[15]

Necessary to keep a countdown of how soon his constituents can replace him?

Rep. Howard Berman spends $84,000 on personalized calendars printed by the U.S. Capitol Historical Society for all of his constituents. Combine that with the $35,280 for postage and you really have to question the worthiness of this expenditure. I think he's just trying to do his part to help the Post Office turn a profit.

So he could take pictures while flying in those private jets?

Ohio Rep. Michael Turner purchased a digital camera to the tune of $1,435. He probably needed it to take pictures while flying around the country on a private jet!

Again I proffer the concept that our vote is the only "police force" available to us for correcting and stopping these abuses. They obviously lack the skills, honesty or desire to police themselves so we have to do it. Somehow we must become shareholders in our government since there is no respect accorded to those who are merely taxpayers which doesn't allow for any special considerations or right to know.

Remember one thing; it is not the amount of money involved but rather the practice which they see as appropriate that we must stop. Take care of the billions and the trillions will fall in place! It's a "New Era of Responsibility" so there should be no expenditures considered off limits. We should all be concerned and offended with the belief by politician's that we lack the intelligence and ability to see beyond them to what is really going on.

---

14 Online.wsj.com/article/SB124364352135868189.html "Lawmakers Bill Taxpayers For TVs, Cameras, Lexus

15 Online.wsj.com/article/SB124381530535870685.html "Lawmakers Keep Expenses Off-Line

Chapter 6

Congressional Alzheimer's

Perhaps I am the first to diagnose the disease but it has been around since the transition from volunteer governing to the concept of the professional politician.

With symptoms that only reveal themselves when actions are held up to light, it is a disease with regional characteristics. It seems only to strike within the boundaries of Washington D.C and only those who attempt to abuse their power. All too often they are found to be making decisions that only enrich themselves or their supporters.

The afflicted struggle with memory lapses of actions they have taken, such as Senator Dodd who couldn't seem to recall, while in front of the television cameras, language in the TARP Bill which allowed AIG to pay their Employee Retention Bonuses. It is a vicious disease that all too often causes recollections to change daily if not hourly.

The next day as it turned out Sen. Dodd did put that language into the bill but could not recall who had pressured him to insert it. (See Chapter 5 "Better to Lie than Take Responsibility")

Senator Obama who pushed for the Earmark to build a plant in Illinois for the study of clean burning coal technologies, said as President, he would not sign the Stimulus Bill if this earmark resurfaced in the legislation. But it did and he did! Closer attention will be required to make sure that these symptoms don't accelerate and become more prevalent.

Now President Obama has evidently also failed to recall that Sen. Durbin, his colleague from Illinois, was one of those helping him with the original earmark. But Sen. Durbin was evidently unaware of or just couldn't remember the hard stance taken by the President on this bill and he inserted it into the Stimulus bill.

It prevents members of congress from remembering that they partake in the very behavior they vilify others for. It prevents them from remembering who they work for, whose money they are spending and how much of it we have or don't have. It convinces them that it's none of our business in spite of the fact that it is us they are supposed to be protecting .It renders them unable to recall exactly what home improvements the oil company did for them on their personal homes. Or just exactly what the behind the scenes benefits were to that special Countrywide mortgage.

An action such as paying $4,500 for $500 junk cars using taxpayer money suddenly makes perfect sense. Borrowing money from China and then turning around and donating it back to China for their Green Building Technology Program! That's right; we borrowed the money from them, added it to our deficit and are paying them interest for the use of the money.

On August 6, 2009 it was disclosed, most likely by one of the non-profit foundations that monitor the behavior of Congress, who had inserted into the Defense Appropriations Bill a line item authorizing the purchase of what turned out to be 8 new Gulfstream Jets to the tune of $550 Million for the traveling convenience of members of congress. It is another example of "Do As Say, Not As I Say Do" but it also serves as further proof of "Congressional Alzheimer's."

Within a few days this item was removed from the bill, however by then the demonstration of the disease had already been exposed by the light. But making it public proved the incredible value of "Transparency" and making their actions stand within the light of day.

Perhaps instead of purchasing new we should just repossess the jets we already own through the automakers and banks we bailed out!

Congressional Alzheimer's is an insidious disease causing all sense of right and wrong to disappear, afflicts their ability to apply common sense to our problems, render's them unable to recognize and understand hypocrisy or recognize the lunacy of their actions. Dangerous and scary it is a disease for which the only known cure is the power of our votes!

Chapter 7

Welcome Aboard Hypocrisy Airlines!

Hypocrisy Airlines is a fleet of government jets maintained and operated by the Air Force out of Andrew's Air force base. It is a fleet made up of various types, sizes, operating ranges (because you surely shouldn't be inconvenienced with a refueling stop en-route) and capacities whose sole purpose is to stand at the ready for the convenience of our elected and administration officials. It only takes a phone call to tell them when and where you would like to go, how many people in your party, what you require for food and refreshments and any other special needs you might have. And don't worry about the cost we will simply bill them to the American Taxpayer and they will pay for it because they don't know any better!

It is another glaring example of how we have allowed the bizarre to become the norm. When did we give our elected officials the okay to define the entitlements they should receive and why we should pay for them? Give them a million and they'll take a billion!

Post 9/11 the decision was made, and under the circumstances probably rightfully so, that for security reasons the Speaker of the House, being second in line to the Presidency after the Vice President, should travel on secure government transport. Okay that makes sense, but 10 years after 9/11 we have had no terrorist attacks on our soil threatening the continuity of the Presidency, yet the practice not only still exists, but has grown to unbelievable levels of entitlement.

The current Speaker of the House, Nancy Pelosi, uses this entitlement to make as many as three round trips to San Francisco each week. First, why so many trips; would there be as many if she had to fly commercial? Second, though she didn't request it, she is provided with a jet with enough range that she isn't impositioned by a refueling stop. Though she didn't request it, the request actually came from the House Sergeant at Arm's; she didn't refuse the larger jet which surely has a greater operating cost than a smaller one would have.

This is another blatant example of how once something is started in Washington D.C it can never be revisited to see if it is still necessary and that it grows beyond anything that was intended with the initial decision. It made sense after 9/11 but is it really necessary today and if so, at what cost?

Ever wondered about all of the "fact finding missions" taken by our elected officials and members of their staff to Iraq and Afghanistan? How much does it cost us to have the necessary flight crews on standby, the purchase, operation, maintenance of this fleet of jets and the military crew that must be onboard each of these flights. Another expense paid little attention is the military flight crew required plus all of the ground personnel required for operation of this fleet?

Darn it! There it is again! Taxpayer not Shareholder

Though we don't know the total number of trips or costs associated with these missions, because they choose not to reveal these costs for fear of public scrutiny, there does seem to be an identifiable assumption we can make about these trips; there just doesn't seem to be any facts to be learned in Iraq or Afghanistan. Or is it that they just aren't smart enough to find them?

I draw this conclusion from the simple fact that we don't seem to be one step closer today than we were 5 or 6 years ago to ending either of these wars. Oh by the way, I didn't have to travel anywhere to reach this conclusion! I just watch the news. I'd say maybe we should buy them televisions for their offices. I'm sorry but I forgot for a moment that according to my research, they not only have TV's, but most of them have flat- screens. I'm hoping that this book will sell really well so that I can get one.

Imagine if the funds for these little junkets, as they so affectionately call them, had been redirected into the military budget for purchase of safety equipment like flack jackets or additional armament on the Humvee's or technology to detect road side bombs before they explode in an effort to protect what should be our greatest asset, the men and women that we have put in harms way.

I've never owned a jet, maybe you have, but I don't think you need to own one to realize not only how much they cost to purchase but also to operate and maintain. To think that there is a fleet of jets, all different shapes and sizes, makes you wonder just how much of our money is used for this privilege. Is it really necessary? And am I incorrect in my perception that all of these flights tend to end in the land of the idiots?

We have commercial airlines that can fly you just about anywhere you might want to go on just about any schedule. These companies are struggling to make a profit in today's economy and maybe as part of the huge stimulus package we should demand that these elite members of "the entitlement club" start to live like the rest of us. I'm not an economist, if I was maybe I would be rich enough to own a jet, but I have to believe that it would be cheaper in the long run even if they flew first class, something else I've never done. Maybe we should learn from the car companies and sell our jets too.

Lest you think I am playing favorites on this subject I now point out that the same holds true with the attitude toward and the use of Air force One. While I know that it is the call sign of whatever plane the President is on, to most of us it means the 747 and that is what I am referring to when I talk about Presidential air travel.

While we all know that it isn't possible for the President to travel any other way I still believe that there needs to be an attitude change as to how that plane is used. In May the President traveled to Las Vegas for a campaign fundraiser for Senator Harry Reid. As you will note in another chapter of this book I have issues with the campaigning habits of our Presidents past, present and future because of the costs we incur as taxpayers. This particular trip cost an estimated $200,000 and that is just flight time costs. How much of this expense is reimbursed by the Party of the candidate? Everything I read suggests that it is the cost of a coach ticket for the same flight on a commercial airline.

I don't know about you but I will tell you right now that I am willing to fly on Air Force One any time for the cost of a coach ticket. It doesn't even have to be the 747, I'd be willing to pay the same cost for a Gulfstream! Want to come fly with me?

I understand the difficulties of Presidential travel but here is my really big question; if it is fair and justified why won't they disclose the true cost? It isn't just fuel but all of the secret service details required both in the air and on the ground and the cost for local law enforcement at the destination as well as the disruption of traffic to accommodate his presence and protect his safety. Plus you need to remember that wherever Air Force One goes it is accompanied by its twin747, by huge cargo planes to accommodate the ground vehicles necessary to get him form his plane to the destination.

During the 8 years of the Bush Presidency how many trips to Crawford and Kennebunkport did Air Force One make? Was it really necessary or could a smaller, less expensive to operate plane have been used. Was it really necessary to have Air Force One sitting at the local airport in order for the President to be prepared to handle a situation that might arise while he was taking one of his many vacations?

The same can be said of the recent stop in Paris at the end of his Middle East tour. Wife and kids were flown to Paris on the Friday night to meet up with him. This took a separate jet and everything that must accompany that jet. So what did it really cost us? How are we supposed to feel when as of April 25th we are operating on borrowed money?

Mrs. OBama and their daughters then stayed on in Paris and then went on to London before returning home. The President returned on Sunday aboard Air Force One.

I was also bothered by the reasoning behind flying them to Paris to meet up with him. "I had them meet me in Paris because neither of my daughters has ever been to Europe." I would like to point out that, while we paid for this special flight so they could finally see Europe, I have never been to Europe and if I ever get there I don't think it will be on a private jet! Couldn't they have skipped a couple days of school and gone as a family on one plane?

Again I can't get past the additional costs and I am losing my confidence in the "New ERA of Responsibility." I don't know about where you live but where I live there are a lot of homeless children who will likely never see Europe either. In fact they would be happy to have a place to live and know that they were going to be able to eat today and maybe tomorrow. What bothers me is the cavalier attitude of entitlement. If things are to really change in this country it is time the government look at all manners of expenditure not just the ones that don't affect their lives.

There are a lot of expenses involved with Presidential travel and I feel like more attention should be given to the necessity of this travel. I am concerned with the attitude of entitlement that Washington D.C. seems to breed regardless of intentions. At $60,000 - $70,000 an hour just in operating costs of Air Force One I can't help but feel that we should expect more thought or maybe it's respect. Take your family with you. I think most Blue Collar people would be fine with that. But to tell us it is acceptable to incur the additional costs is being unreasonable and not the change we were looking for. When you decide you want the top job in the world and you attain it there should be more thought given to the things that maybe you will have to give up. Maybe it is time that the President needs to think about less travel to minimize the expenditures. After all we asked the UAW workers and retirees to rethink their compensation and privileges.

Don't read this as OBama bashing because that is not my intention. In fact I think that President Bush was probably the biggest abuser of entitlement that has been in the White House in a long time. I just say we should be respected. We are all being asked to sacrifice and be patient while the government attempts to resolve the current recession so our elected officials should be expected to do the same.

Chapter 8

What does History Tell Us About Pork Barrel Spending?

According to Nevada Senator Harry Reid "it has been around since we were a country." That this should be justification enough to practice stealing from the National Treasury to satisfy their personal interests would seem to me not to be able to hold up under light of day.

Idaho Senator Larry Craig and Idaho Rep. Mike Simpson would have us believe that "eliminating earmarks would equate to an unconstitutional delegation of spending discretion to the executive branch." A rather disappointing argument when you consider all of the time Sen. Craig spends in public restrooms practicing his toe tapping routines. Couldn't some of that time be spent coming up with a better defense for the theft of the Treasury? [16] And did not the Constitution grant the spending powers to the States? So maybe he should spend his time in the stall reading the Constitution.

It is true that pork barrel spending requests have been around since we were a country; but let's take a look at how our founding fathers responded to such requests.[17]

"The First Congress rejected a bill to loan money to a glass manufacturer after several members challenged the constitutionality of the proposal. In a debate in the second Congress over a bill to pay a bounty to New England Cod fisherman, Rep. Hugh Williamson of South Carolina argued that it was unconstitutional "to gratify one part of the Union by oppressing the other...destroy this barrier; and it is not

---

16   www.senate.gov/~craig/releases/ed020106a.htm

17   CAGW "All about pork: The Abuse of Earmarks and the Needed Reform"

a few fisherman that will enter, but all manner of persons; people of every trade and occupation may enter the breach, until they have eaten up the bread of our children."[18]

Today's "Gatekeeper" through this barrier would have to be Rep. John Murtha. Few who have crossed this barrier have not first had to pay homage, financially and with votes for his chosen special interests, to John Murtha. In a nutshell Rep. Hugh Williamson was stating that, once breached, every business under the sun would come to the Federal Government looking for bailouts until our Treasury was empty. Compare this prediction to where we are today and you have to wonder at the abilities of the Founding Fathers to predict human nature.

If I understand correctly, the treasury is empty but it doesn't stop those who see themselves as Rulers from continuing to spend as though this weren't the case.

In 1822 President James Monroe argued that federal money should be limited "to great national works only, since if it were unlimited it would be liable to abuse and might be productive of evil." Seems rather prescient now doesn't it?

Again, were they prescient or just excellent predictors of human nature? Sen. Harry Reid must not have spent much time in history class; otherwise he would have a better handle on the fact that the requests have indeed been around since "we were a country" but in the opinions of our forefathers allowing such a system could only lead to abuse, corruption and the bankrupting of our country. Times may be different today, we are a large country with a much broader responsibility to our citizens, but the basic tenets of human nature are as true today as they were 233 years ago. Sen. Larry Craig's concern is that he wouldn't be able to protect his re-election without the constant use of pork to protect his incumbency.

Our forefathers envisioned a system whereby Congress "would fund general grant programs and let the federal and state agencies select individual recipients through a competitive process or formula."[19] In other words Congress wouldn't pick winners and losers, they would be chosen by the people who best knew the issues and values

18   John C Eastman "Eating Up the Bread of Our Children" www.claremont.org/projects/jurisprudence/060206eastman.html

19   CAGW "All about pork: The Abuse of Earmarks and the Needed Reform"

of the various programs requesting funding. Today's system is one of members of Congress, constantly surpassing the breadth of their knowledge, picking the winners and losers. These decisions are based on the position and power they individually hold and rarely have any correlation to the importance of these winners to society as a whole. The erected procedures of Congress are easily subverted with the use of "Pork."

> "The same prudence which in private life would forbid
> our paying our own money for unexplained projects,
> forbids it in the dispensation of the public's money."
>
> Thomas Jefferson

I would offer up examples such as "FutureGen" in Chicago, the Congressional bike program for members and staffers in Washington D.C, to smoke or not to smoke marijuana at WA State Univ., Alaska's train to nowhere, International Storytelling Center in Tennessee, the 16.8 million dollars awarded to a Wisconsin foodbank for purchase of "canned ham," supporting the church of one member of Congress with a special pork bill or the billions given to businesses in 2009.

Article 1 Section 8 of the U.S. Constitution has been hijacked by our elected Representatives today for what they call the "power of the purse" claiming it was the intention of the Founding Fathers that only congress could spend the taxpayers money and that it is only they who have the qualifications to determine how that money is spent. The only possible explanation for this demented and indefensible interpretation of the Founding Fathers is "Congressional Alzheimer's."

So what does history tell us about pork barrel spending? That it was not the intention of the Founding Fathers when they granted the "power of the purse" to Congress that monies would be stolen from the Treasury to satisfy the demands of special interest nor was it intended to allow the use as political capital to protect the positions of incumbent members, serve their own personal interests or the interests of their constituents.

In these times of extreme economical and financial stress it is more important than ever that we find a way to require proper Stewardship over our money. If history is to be our teacher we desperately need people in power who have the ability to relearn the principles set forth by the Founding Fathers. We can no longer allow Stewardship be defined by the size and amount of the misuse, if it circumnavigates the system it is embezzlement pure and simple. If it were a public corporation the use of our money by our government could only be classified as "embezzlement." We need to eliminate the practice to cure the disease.

Two hundred million dollars being inserted into the 2009 Defense Appropriations bill for the purchase of 2 Gulfstream jets for the traveling convenience of members of Congress illustrates how little these lawmakers understand history or the definition of Hypocrisy. Belittling of corporate CEO's about the use of private jets and then using our money to pay for their own convenience when traveling displays exactly the attitude of "better than thou" that exists in Washington. They flaunt their own rules, they change the rules when it benefits them and they continue to try to subvert transparency by burying the evidence of their actions where it makes it all but impossible to ferret out the information.

Their behavior can be succinctly summed up in the immortal words of John Murtha when questioned about his lack of disclosure "so you have to work for the information, tough shit!" This is our representation ladies and gentleman and their opinion of our right to be involved in our government.

Our forefathers lived under control of the Ruling Class and our Independence is a direct result of that experience. The design of the United States of America was developed to assure that the control of the government remain in the hands of the governed. That we would never live under the control of a Ruler. We now are faced with a government that is no longer Representative of the will of the people, decisions no longer made for the betterment of society but for the special few and the stewardship of our assets and resources is none existent.

Chapter 9

Better to Lie Than Take Responsibility

I was taught that it is better to state the truth, take your punishment and move on. The problem with lies is that they are hard to keep track of and they can lead down some very precarious pathways. Especially if you suffer from Congressional Alzheimer's!

For example;

Had Former President Clinton been honest at the outset about his relationship with Monica Lewinski the American People would probably have been outraged for a short time but it would most likely have passed and never gone to hearings on impeachment.

Just think of all of the cases of adultery by other holders of public office from senators to state governors that have made the news during the first half of 2009. Even though we feel outrage and disappointment in their behavior how many will really fail to be re-elected in the next election cycle? It would seem that the only one that really affected the House and Senate Ethics Committee's sensibilities is Senator Larry Craig. Maybe if he had of been in the ladies restroom they would have felt better about it.

Had the issue of the presence of "WMD's" in Iraq been handled truthfully we probably wouldn't have ended up in a war that has cost us thousands of American lives and that has virtually bankrupted our economy to say nothing of what we have done to the infrastructure of Iraq or the number of Iraqi citizens who have lost their lives, homes and careers.

It's like a shell game where the truth is under one of a hundred shells and we have to try to determine which shell it is. Put enough misdirection out there and the odds that we will find the truth go way down. It is the same misdirection used by David Copperfield when he makes the Statue of Liberty or a Boeing 747 disappear. Logic tells us they are still there but we can't see them. Senator Dodd seems to be the biggest proponent of this process.

Honesty seems to not have a place in American politics anymore. Too many of our elected officials seem to operate under the mistaken belief that you can fool all of the people all of the time. Of course you can't lump them all into this category because that would be a lie too, but too many think it is in their job descriptions and that we will swallow it hook line and sinker. It really comes back to a total lack of respect for the ability of Blue Collar people to reason through the things we are told and expected to accept with no questions asked.

"Just trust us, the money to pay for Health Care Insurance Reform will be there when needed!" If that is the truth why can't you collect it all together so we can see it before you start spending more? If it is written as an excise tax in the Health Care Insurance Reform bill then why can't you just admit honestly that "Yes it is a tax?"

At the end of the movie Man of the Year, Robin Williams states that "politicians are like diapers, they should be changed often and for the same reasons." I don't think there has ever been a more accurate assessment of our politicians.

Some of them lie to the American People through the television camera, some through omission, some through intentional non-disclosure but most through a combination of all of these ways. Look at the process of creating the budget; if a department doesn't want to fund a program but a politician knows it will create job losses, or have a negative impact on one of the special interests they owe and make them the target of ridicule, they will simply reinsert these programs into the budget as a "Pork Barrel Spending" amendment. And even though there are transparency laws which have been in place since 2007 many politicians still lack the courage, or truly believe they are exempt, to identify themselves as the author.

Rep. Bobby Rush and the earmark for the church he founded, Sen. Dodd and Sen. Kent Conrad and their Countrywide mortgage's, Sen. Murtha and his continual earmarking for his personal special interests, and Nancy Pellosi quietly behind the scenes securing support for Democrats who need the political capital to protect their tenure.

House Ways and Means Committee Chairman Charles Rangel who couldn't remember receiving any rental income on investment properties he owned nor the fact that he didn't recall having 4 rent controlled properties leased in Harlem, But he was cognizant enough to keep his adjusted gross income on his tax returns just below the maximum allowable for rent controlled units. But he is surviving under the protection of the leadership.

Rulers are not subject to the incriminations of their actions, they reside above the laws of man and God and they serve up their own version of what the truth is. Representatives are those we chose to send forth to represent the interests of all citizens but to often Rulers are what we end up with even though it sacrifices the good of the all. We need a "New Era of Responsibility" but until we can put control of the government back in the hands of the people it will never be more than a dream.

These are just a few examples of those who never forget who they owe and never shy away from gaining political capital by abusing the system and the trust of their constituents. Each has been given their personal chapters in order to expound on their behaviors.

Chapter 10

What does "Transparency" really mean?

Defined as something which is made visible by the "Light Behind It" there was an attempt made to remove the veil of secrecy from the Pork Barrel process. The Federal Funding Accountability and Transparency Act of 2006 was signed into law By President Bush on September 26, 2006 but not without the last minute attempts by Senators Stevens and Byrd, whose careers are defined by their love for the other white meet, to block it from coming to a vote in the Senate.

Using a little known tool called, what else, "The Secret Hold" they attempted to prevent the bill from reaching a vote in the Senate. This is another tool, and how many more are there, protecting anonymity of the requestor. Their move was eventually blocked through the efforts of Senator Coburn, the blog Porkbusters, GOPProgress.com and TPMuckraker.com. The two Senators were identified and confronted bringing their authorship into the public light forcing these two porkers to admit their involvement and release the hold.

This new legislation required very specific steps required for every item of "Pork Barrel" spending including;

> Authorship
> Dollar Amount of request
> Purpose of the request
> End Recipient of the of the funds
> Parent Entity of the Recipient
> Other Information as Deemed Relevant by the Office
> of Management and Budget

So why did the Fiscal year 2008/2009 budget contained 10,160 "Pork" bills totaling expenditures of 11.8 billion dollars? Curiously, of this total 221 failed to disclose authorship of the bills. While these 221 bills only make up .022% of the total number of pork passed into law without debate or justification, they represented a total of 7.8 billion dollars or 66% of the $11.8 billion expenditure.[20]

So why are they so difficult to find in the budget? Why were they accepted without the disclosure of all the items required by the legislation? In January 2007, the rules from the original bill were dissolved into a requirement only that the requesting member post the innocuous letter on their website stating that they requested it but received no personal gain by sponsoring. It removed the rest of the public disclosure requirements listed above. The only way to define this action is that it is nothing more than the bait and switch used by most Con Men. By taking the bite out of the original legislation they are now in the position of again perpetuating the secrecy and lack of disclosure.

So who has taken advantage of it? All members of Congress, with the exception of the few like Senators Coburn and McCain who don't request Pork, from Senate and House leadership down through the ranks to the very bottom. It is a definite move by our elected officials to directly thumb their noses at the Blue Collar voters letting us know who is really in charge and that they will never be answerable to the voters for their actions.

Look at Senator Reids' $5,000,000 for research, development, testing and evaluation of Single Generator Operations Lithium Ion Batteries which was later revealed to have been awarded, outside of any public debate or open bidding process to Altair Nanotechnologies of Reno, NV. No disclosure of recipient or purpose for the award.[21]

But he isn't alone! Senator Mitch McConnell and $4,000,000 for Bio/Nano-EMS for defense Applications. And his chosen winner, because there was no public competition from the day he wrote the bill, turned out to be the University of Louisville.

Of course there was no identifying information released until much

---

20 Citizens Against Government Waste 2009 Pigbook

21 Taxpayers for common Sense "Senate Guts Earmark Transparency Rules"

later when it became to late to stop the projects. This is all to often how the process works; you simply keep your actions in the dark until such time as the project can't be stopped. Then and only then do you allow it to be exposed to public analysis.

In "Transparency and Open Government"[22] President Obama states, "my administration is committed to creating an unprecedented level of openness in government. We will work together to ensure the public trust and establish a system of transparency, public participation and collaboration. Openness will strengthen our democracy and promote efficiency and effectiveness in Government."

The dream of all dreams! But as long as the prevailing attitude is that it is better to ignore the input of those who are governed and do what best serves your interests. If we don't support the President in the 2010 election cycle by removing those who will and do fight the notion of Transparency be they Democrat, Republican or Independent the dream will always remain just out of reach. The time has come that we have to start looking not at party but at individual members, and deduce from their behaviors do they conduct themselves as Representatives or Rulers.

We are climbing a massive amount of debt. How can there be any glimmers of hope that we can retire this debt if we cannot even stop our elected officials from stealing our money to feed their ego's, political debts and other self interests?

It was suppose to be available now to answer all of our questions

There was a promise of transparency made by President Obama that assured us that we would be able to follow every dime of the $787 billion Stimulus Bill. And now they are allocating another $1.8 billion to redesign the Recovery.gov website and another year or more to complete it and make the information available. I've seen teenagers build websites in days.

Now the leadership is fighting a move to post the Healthcare bill online for 72 hours before their vote. This illustrates their intention of transparency. If they were to post it we would be able to see there is a "Pork" bill already inserted by Sen. Tom Harkin, "under the guise of

---

22 www.whitehouse.gov/the _press_office/Transparency_andOpenGovernment

prevention and wellness,"[23] for $10 billion to build bike trails, jungle gyms, farmers markets and lighting.

Are they sure it is the "New Era of Responsibility" they promised us?

---

23 www.onenewsnow.com

Chapter 11

The Perfect Example of What is Wrong With Politics Today!

Senator Christopher Dodd on March 18, 2009[24] stands on the steps of the Senate Building, looks into the camera and states that he has no idea how the language protecting the AIG retention pay contracts were put into the TARP bill.

But the next day, March 19th, he is trapped into admitting the truth that he and his staff were the ones that put the language in. So he goes into defense mode, laying as many shells as he can onto the table in a lame attempt to hide the truth. He states "let me be clear, I was completely unaware of these AIG bonuses until I learned of them last week."

But didn't he just say the day before, in the video, that he knew nothing about the language being in the bill? Now he tells us he knew about the AIG Bonuses the prior week. Then he states that he was adamant that this language not be in the bill, but didn't he just say the day before that he knew nothing? Now he was adamant that the language be included. Wasn't it his explanation that it was at the behest of the administration or treasury?

He then stated that he had no idea that the language would affect AIG, but if he actually read the bill shouldn't he have been able to figure it out? So what he is really telling us is that he doesn't take the time to read the bills he votes for. Is that what he was sent to Washington to do?

---

24 View the video of the interview at www.cnn.com/2009/POLITICS/03/18/aig. bonuses.congress/index.html?iref=newssearch#cnnSTCVideo

Yesterday he simply had no knowledge of how it got in there, but what a difference of 24 hours makes, today it turns out it was his office, but it was everybody else's fault that the language was left in the bill. He received pressure from the staff at the Treasury Dept. or pressure from the White House. He couldn't remember quite who it was that applied the pressure.

He went on to say that he was concerned that the public is losing trust in their legislators' ability to deal with these issues. In all of our legislators or just the ones who lie to us? Wow, do you think?

If you look at the video he should remind you of the little kid lying to one of his parents but the parent keeps questioning until the truth, usually inadvertently, comes to the surface. Then it becomes, "yeah I did it" but it was his fault or her fault or I didn't know any better. In the video he talks to how "confusion was caused by my explanation yesterday" but don't lies by their very nature cause confusion?

Congressional Alzheimer's prevented him from remembering the specifics even though only 48 hours had passed. Another symptom of this vicious disease is an unexplainable love for Teflon coating.

Lack of disclosure, also a form of lying, is a huge problem with Washington D.C. and Sen. Christopher Dodd appears to hold a PHD in this subject.

When the mortgage crisis began to become public in September 2008 one of the things that came to light was what is called the "Friends of Mizulo" mortgage programs. Angelo Mizulo, founder of Country Wide Home Loans gave special consideration, rates and fees to selected influential people within our government as well as other corporate executives in a position to help him at some future time in the operation of his company.

It came to light that Sen. Dodd was a beneficiary of this program on his mortgage of approximately $850,000 for a personal residence as well as another for an investment property. This type of mortgage would typically have an interest rate (called jumbo rates) which is higher than the conforming rates you typically hear about. In addition there would be 2% to 3% in fees involved with this mortgage amount or $17,000 to $25,500 and could be even higher depending on personal information concerning income, assets etc.

We had testimony provided by the Countrywide loan officer which revealed 2 items of special interest. First that Sen. Dodd received at least a one point discount on one of his loans which was valued at approximately $10,500 and second that it was made perfectly clear to him that it was a special deal. Dodds' action to make amends? He made a charitable contribution of this amount which he feels should exonerate him from any wrong doing or any appearance of monetary benefit.

However this is a pretty flimsy way to prove his innocence. It still does not discount the fact that he was offered and accepted special consideration. In loans of this type it is most common that the closing costs associated with a loan are rolled into the new loan amount and you pay interest on those costs over the length of the loan. However in Sen. Dodd's case that is not the result, which means that he still will save a tremendous amount of money from this special treatment.

On September 28, 2009 it was disclosed that there were actual tapes of the conversations which revealed that each recipient of the "Friends of Mizulo" program were made aware of the benefits they were receiving. These conversations were between the Countrywide loan officers and those clients who benefited. Alas though, they were somehow destroyed after it was made public just who benefited.

Perhaps rather than the title of senator he is more qualified to hold the title of Dr. of Misdirection and Non-disclosure! In reality if you watch the complete video or read the transcript he would tell the lie and in the next breath give us a new explanation which proved the previous statement was another lie. Can he really be that disconnected from even his own words? Perhaps he knows what we should have figured out by now; he doesn't have a clue!

Ultimately the voters of Connecticut will have to make the final diagnosis of whether he is an outright liar, in which case why would they send him back, or is he so ill that he needs to be removed from office to protect against his future decline in memory and overall health?

There is also evidence now, which came out during the testimony of the Countrywide loan officer, that North Dakota Senator Kent Conrad was also the recipient of a "Friends of Mizulo" mortgage for an apartment building in which special concessions were made. The loan he received should have been commercial because the property exceeded the unit size for a conforming loan. He maintains his innocence while at the same time refusing to disclose loan papers that would exonerate him. Did he study under Senator Dodd?

Sen. Dodd has been in the news a lot over the past 6 or 8 months which has made it easy for me to use him as an example. Part of what this book is about however, is what should be expected of our elected officials. The point being that he chose to lie to us rather than give us the truth and take the appropriate responsibility for his actions. I think we can also assume at this point that he surely isn't alone. So should we accept this as business as usual? Or is it time for us to call them on their lies and use our votes to show them it is unacceptable behavior going forward?

You can't change the rules on an old dog!

Shifting political realities force Dodd to try to change his stripes only to find out that those stripes are skin deep. After 28 years as a special friend of lobbyists and special interests he now wants a divorce. The new strategy is to yell, scream and belittle them even though they have continued to provide financial support for his re-election, some 38% to be more precise. Of course these special interests are from the same industries, health care and financial services, which currently have business before his committees. Paid protection for personal profit has always been the name of his game so what are the odds.

After all these years of keeping him in power they are now the arch villain. Loyalty evidently not being in his vocabulary you have to wonder, if re-elected, what will make him loyal to the needs of his constituents? Isn't it more likely that the day after the election will see the old stripes resurface?

August 7, 2009 the Senate Ethics Committee completed the investigation into the mortgages from Countrywide and published their finding that "while no illegal benefits were gained both Senators should have exercised greater caution to prevent unintended benefits." This decision only serves to draw emphasis to the problem of members conducting investigations against their own colleagues. There was really no expectation that any different finding could have been expected.

Chapter 12

They Call This Leadership?

It may have taken us 8 years but we've learned the expensive lesson of electing a "C" student to the Presidency. But how much longer can we put off the lessons of leadership which is morally, ethically and honesty void.? How much longer are we to accept the behavior which has bankrupted this country. Not just financially but also our reputation.

The United States is the largest corporation on earth and if we were publicly traded we would have already been declared insolvent. The SEC and every other branch of our government would be trying and imprisoning the board of directors. You can only describe the stewardship of our treasury as the biggest embezzlement in history. In fact it puts the likes of Bernie Madoff into the petty cash category.

And yet the spending continues. The pump no longer finding water in the well now pumps sand to the surface and yet they continue to spend. Perhaps we can start repaying the holders of our debt in sand dollars!

Speaker Pelosi, even though seeing the Republicans swept from office over undisciplined spending and the continued practice of pork spending, sits as an umbrella of protection over the largest pork farmer of them all; John Murtha. Why does she protect him even though he continues to steal from the treasury? Political debt would seem to be the explanation. She attributes a large portion of her rise through the system to the help and mentoring of Mr. Murtha. So the payback is on. It isn't enough for our politicians to owe their special interests and supporters, they also have to owe each other.

It is quite obvious to the Blue Collar people of this country that John Murtha needs to be dealt with through investigation and prosecution. Unfortunately his prosecution would probably be handled by our Justice dept. in much the same way they handled Sen. Stevens, who was not acquitted, but rather charges were dropped because of all of the legal mistakes and abuses committed by our Justice Dept.

Nancy Pelosi and the situation with the CIA over torture makes you question the validity of anything our leaders have to say. If her original stance was correct in saying that she was never informed of waterboarding techniques being used, why not stop there? Instead her recollection changed several times over the next couple of weeks and it came down to the simple fact that the "CIA lies to Congress all the time." Interestingly enough what she is really inferring in this statement is that Congress hates to be lied to! But Ms. Pelosi isn't that what you do to the constituents on a regular basis?

Speaker Pelosi and Senator Hoyer I have a news alert for you. You were elected to represent the will of the people not to rule over us as if you were a dictator and we your subjects. We are tired of being lied to, called un-American for speaking out, and my personal favorite, accused of giving our approval for violence and assassination through our rhetoric.

Typically when a politician reacts this way to the criticism of the citizens it's because we are getting to close to the truth and, in the words of Jack Nicholson, "you can't handle the truth!"

Senator Harry Reid, whose behavior is deficient in so many ways, has made the choice to turn down the request that Congress investigate the Democrat leaning organization Acorn stating that "...it would distract from efforts to address health care, climate change, overhauling of the nation's financial regulatory system and oversight of the wars in Iraq and Afghanistan." Evidently these issues are worth far more to us than stopping Acorn from getting any more tax dollar grants. Sure they halted the 8.5 billion dollars set aside in the Stimulus Bill but unfortunately that is not the only way they receive their funding. But what the hell it's only taxpayer money!

Our government is not a dictatorship but it's hard to remember this when our leadership fails to understand the difference between right and wrong. Leadership is not about protecting those who abuse the system for their own personal gain. It is about exposing corruption within the organization and eliminating it. It is hard to take serious the accusations and abuse heaped upon the corporate world for their actions when you hold your umbrella of protection over the worst of the worst.

Failing to take action against the likes of John Murtha, Bobbie Rush, Christopher Dodd and Ted Stevens, to name just a few, you lack the credibility to criticize others. Until you police your own houses you certainly are not qualified to police the houses of others. I think it's called "removing the log from your own eye before removing the splinter from the eye of another."

Leadership is about taking responsibility, exercising honesty, morals and ethics in your own behavior, making the tough decisions regardless of the potential cost to your incumbency or the debts you have accumulated to special interests and colleagues. Our leadership has the weight of responsibility upon them to do the will of the people regardless of the consequences to those who helped them reach their position. Leadership should be a beacon of example to those they lead.

As citizens we have power over the only remedy available, the use of our vote. When they demonstrate that they no longer represent but rule over our citizens it is our duty, placed upon us by the founding fathers, to exercise the policing powers of that vote to remove those who would abuse us. In other words we no longer have to put up with this behavior and we do indeed deserve the respect of our representatives.

Chapter 13

Rangel (ing) over the definition of truth and lie!

One thing you have to give poor old Charlie is credit for consistency. Four decades in Congress has seen a trail of deceit, special entitlement, real estate manipulations and tax fraud fill the wake of his career. To be sure he has done positive things for his constituents in Harlem, but should that absolve him of responsibility for this long history of ethics and tax violations? Here is a man who sits at the head of the House Ways and Means Committee which, among other things, writes the Internal Revenue Service laws. Shouldn't this position hold him to a higher standard of conduct? He consistently blames "the right wing media" for continuing to attempt to destroy him so lets go back four decades and take a look at what he would have us believe is manufactured truths.

During his first campaign in 1970 it was brought to light that several years earlier he had taken out a $39,000 loan to rehabilitate his childhood home. The money was lent through a New York City low income housing program at an interest rate below market which was subsidized by the organization. The house was converted into six apartments which were then to be rented to low income residents. But he continued to occupy one unit, in violation of the terms of the loan. So was Charlie really your typical low income person?

He later went on to justify the deal by claiming that "I wasn't a public official when I took that loan." So the fact that he failed to follow the terms of the loan doesn't matter because he wasn't the Congressman from Harlem then. Even though it is completely irrelevant, let's remember this justification as we look at ethics violations yet to come. Remember over the next forty years he is the Congressman from Harlem.

In 1971 he purchased a home in the Washington D.C. area which he listed as his primary residence. Over the next 30 years he claimed several different tax credits on this property while he actually continued to occupy the apartment in grandma's house In 1989 he borrowed another $60,000 on grandma's old house stating on the application that this was his primary residence even though by this time he had moved into another upscale apartment in Harlem now listed as his primary residence. If that was the case then why did he receive the tax credits for the D.C. home? How did he qualify for the more favorable terms of a mortgage on a primary property when it was really an investment property?

The upscale apartment was two units turned into one large unit and was a rent controlled property. The fact that it was rent controlled meant that your income couldn't exceed approximately $170,000, it has to be your primary residence and you cannot lease more than one unit at a time. But then Charlie, exempt from all rules and regulations, leased another smaller unit on the same floor and in 1999 leased yet another unit which he used for his campaign office.

The count is now one home in D.C. receiving special tax breaks and three rent controlled units in New York. So he is currently standing at four primary residences. Now let's move onto his investment income and properties which could not be listed on his tax returns or his financial disclosure filings because his income would have exceeded the limit for the rent control units not to mention the additional taxes which would have been triggered by full disclosure.

Now it turns out that he failed to disclose some $75,000 rental income on a villa he owns in the Dominican Republic stating "I didn't realize I had any income from this property." For two decades he has been receiving income from this property but somehow he always manages to forget about it at tax time!!! Could there be better evidence of "Congressional Alzheimer's?

Amazingly enough it was calculated that he owed an additional $10,000 in taxes on this income which sounds a little low but that is the amount the IRS said he owed. Though he paid these back taxes he wasn't charged any penalties or interest on this amount which spans almost a decade. Next time you find yourself owing back taxes try telling them you want the Charlie Rangel deal and see how it works out for you. But wait there is even more and it is even scarier!

Somehow he has forgotten about three other properties he owns in New Jersey, an account at the Capital Credit Union containing somewhere between $250,000 and $500,000 as well as an investment account worth somewhere around $500,000. His original 2007 financial disclosure statement reported his worth somewhere between $500,000 and $1.3 million but according to corrected filings in 2009 he was worth somewhere between $1 million and $2.5 million.

So here we have a member of Congress who lost track of approximately 50% of his actual worth. Now, how secure do you feel with him as sitting Chairman over the House Ways and Means Committee? Do you feel safe with representatives like this managing your healthcare? With leadership like this do you really believe that the out of control spending will ever be brought back under control?

Democrat leaders feel that his good has outweighed his bad and given the fact that he had to wait for years to move into the Chairmanship, it would be a unfair to remove him from that position based on the evidence thus far! In the first place you have to wonder at what point is behavior and special entitlement no longer acceptable behavior. You also have to wonder if, by the time the ethics committee, which is made up of his colleagues, completes their investigation, will poor old Charlie still be alive?

Not discussed here are numerous other violations such as using office letterhead for fundraising, receiving special interest free loans and passing tax legislation favoring specific companies while at the same time taking their campaign contributions in excess of a million dollars. In addition he sold grandma's house to a church for $420,000. He then wrote letters in support for the church's application for low income tax breaks as well as tax credits for a nine million dollar apartment renovation project. It also does not include questionable trips to the Caribbean nor his fund raising practices supporting his Charles B. Rangel Center for Public Service in New York

As a Blue Collar person I have to stop and wonder just what an elected member of Congress has to do to warrant disciplinary action for their behavior. If forty years of arrogance and holding oneself above the law of mere Blue Collar people doesn't qualify him for disciplinary action what does? Cheating Charlie's transgressions make Ted Stevens from Alaska look like a beginner but remember he was convicted. Maybe it was just because Stevens was a Republican.

Here is an idea of how to put their skin in the game. Right now when politicians have to defend themselves against ethics charges there is no cost to them. Campaign finance laws allow them to pay all attorneys fees and costs of defense from their campaign contributions. You want them to sit up and take responsibility; change the laws so that they pay their own costs of defense and/or fines from their personal fortunes. Now that would be putting skin in the game which is exactly what they have been calling for from every leader in the bailed out world of corporate America.

I don't know how you were raised but my parents never failed to establish that there would always be a price paid for breaking the rules or that I alone would be the payee. Perhaps treating these politicans like the recalcitrant children they have become would establish a new value on following the rules!

Chapter 14

False Prophet Profits from Earmark Legislation!

"I'm sorry but I have no recollection who authored that earmark." Is it just another case of Congressional Alzheimer's, outright lie in the name of god or a simple case of stealing for God? Whatever description is apropos the lesson to be learned from this earmark is that when God can't or won't do it, just call Rep. Bobby Rush.

Following his god's credence that it is "Better to Lie than Take Responsibility" he refuses to answer questions surrounding a $305,500[25] earmark that went to his church and shows only his name as author. In addition he is unable to recall whether he is a paid member of the staff of this church he founded and isn't sure that they received the money even though he and his wife are Board Members of the church.

It also appears that there is most likely a large family involvement which would make you wonder who else is on the payroll. It should be considered an ethics violation and be subjected to an investigation for the misappropriation of funds. The church, which is supposed to be a non-profit organization should be required to open its books to the ethics committee and then compared with the financial disclosures that the Congressman is legally required to file. A direct comparison would surely expose a failure to report income from the church which is a matter of tax evasion. So not only an embezzler of taxpayer money but also cheating the government out of its income through payment of taxes.

There are also instances of moving campaign contribution money to the church which surely should be illegal. But alas, our leadership

---

25   By September 2009 the new total has risen to well over $400,000 in taxpayer money plus hundreds of thousands in campaign funds redirected to the church.

seems to lack the will to pursue behavior of what surely must be a violation of several laws and embezzlement of the taxpayer money at the very least.

In making a couple of calls to this church I was able to verify that he is in fact the only minister of the church and returns home every weekend to preach. When asked about whether his was a paid position of the church I was immediately hung up on. When told he returns home each weekend I couldn't help but wonder who is paying all of those travel expenses. Unfortunately transparency of Representatives use of their office operating budgets are not yet published for public review but if we could see his I am sure we would find that we are paying his travel expenses with taxpayer money even though he is returning to meet his obligations to the church.

I also discovered that this is one of the few houses of worship which had no website. Every search under the name of the church takes you to a site that shows all of the political and less savory associations Rep. Bobby Rush has with different associations such as the Illinois Chapter of the Black Panthers. Or it simply gives you a map and directions to the church. No mission statement, charities supported or community activism.

This is another blatant case of elected officials not wanting their activities to be brought into the open because they cannot survive public criticism. It shows the belief by too many of their interpretation that they are above the law. Demonstrating a lack of respect or sense of duty to the citizen's, it is nothing more than theft of the taxpayer's dollars for personal benefit and would be classified and prosecuted as embezzlement if it were a public corporation. Unfortunately taxpayers do not seem to be recipients of the same rights as shareholders.

A cautionary point though; stealing is stealing whether it is outright like Bobby Rush, special interests supported by the likes of John Murtha, failure to properly report income and pay appropriate taxes as Rep. Charlie Wrangel, using taxpayer money to payoff political debts or simply getting special treatment on a mortgage because of your position.

Chapter 15

30 Pieces of Silver now Worth $3.5 Billion!

Representative Kaptur Ohio Democrat proves to be nothing more than a modern day Judas. Seeing an opportunity to finally get funding that had been denied her for years, she gets 3.5 billion dollars for an unnecessary federal power authority in Ohio. While even her colleagues in the senate and house and her own constituents say it is a waste of money she forges on. She demonstrates the understanding of the professional politician that if you wait long enough you will be offered your 30 pieces of silver.

Just who are the modern day priests willing to pay for the betrayal of the public trust; non other than House Speaker Nancy Pelosi and House Energy and Commerce Chairman Henry Waxman. Agreed to in secret and slipped into a 300 page amendment to the climate bill delivered to the House for vote at 3:00am without allowing members the opportunity to read the amendment prior to voting, it would deny believability if it weren't so commonplace in how things are done in Washington today. Deliberate deception has become the norm rather than the exception in politics today.

Justification for the price of Rep. Kapturs' betrayal is explained by her spokesman Steve Fought. Seeing the struggling climate-change bill as a vehicle that was strong enough to carry the project into law he states, "when she saw this coming down the pike, she saw an opportunity to attach something she's kicked around for a long time. The inclusion of this in the legislation "made it possible for her to entertain voting for the bill." It was not "THE" factor, but a factor, in her decision to vote for the bill."[26]

---

26 www.washingtontimes.com "Rep. Kaptur gets $3.5 billion sweetener in Climate Bill"

With a system currently in place that serves the needs of its customers quite well and has been doing so for decades this can only be described as bribery by an official for her own benefit. It will do nothing to create new jobs, improve upon what is already in place, benefit the country as a whole nor even the citizens of her own state. This is the kind of behavior that is not only condoned but facilitated by the leadership in both houses of government.

The Cap and Trade Bill is a dubious bill at best which most analysts conclude will fail to deliver any positive affects on global warming but will serve to drive the cost of energy up by several thousand dollars per year for most Americans. While Rep. Kaptur isn't the only Judas in Washington today, she has certainly set the price for betrayal of the public trust at an unfathomable level.

It's a high bar for the cost of a single vote, but when you are using "Monopoly Money" as our politicians seem to think they are spending, no price is evidently too high. But you have to question the value of a bill when you have to buy the votes of your own party to get it to pass!

Chapter 16

Spooning with Pigs!
The John Murtha Political Mating Program

On Febraury 9, 2010 Rep. Murtha passed away. I have struggled with the effect this should have on this chapter. Should I leave it as is? Should I delete it altogether? Or should I pick some middle ground?

My decision is to leave the chapter as originally written for the simple reason that it is representative of the attitude existing in Washington D.C. of entitlement which says they are entitled to do as they please regardless of whether it benefits the citizenry of this country or is simply used to meet political debts to special interests and their own reelection efforts. His passing does not diminish the behaviors demonstrated over a 40 year career or his tendency to take as he pleased from our assets.

A self contained study in all that is wrong with politics today; Murtha has surrounded himself with his own piglet offspring to support the Murtha Family Trust and Special Interest payback system of government. [27] For an eye-opening look at the Murtha form of government, just go to the Citizens of Responsibility and Ethics in Washington website, click on "you don't know jack" and take a quick course in political science the Murtha way. You will also see that nepotism is alive and well in Washington.

With arrogance personified he seems to be saying to the country "Honesty, Integrity and Ethical Behavior" as well as "Transparency and Accountability" be Damned!" They have no place in politics. Here is a revealing truth about the respect he has for the American people and what he truly feels his purpose is.

---

27 http://www.crewsmostcorrupt.org/you-dont-know-jack

"If I am corrupt it's because I take care of my district."
   (that's right he really said "if")
"The "P" in John P. Murtha stands for power."
"I believe that elected representatives of the people
understand their constituents and districts best."

Unfortunately it is at the cost of the citizens of the other 49 states. Done in secret and supposedly under the red, white and blue, he would have us believe he is the only true American concerned with the protection of our troops. In fact he would have us believe he knows better than our own Department of Defense the needs of our military! But the real winners in his system are relatives and those defense contractors located in his district, which encompasses almost all of them. It has nothing to do with the safety of our troops or the need for specific equipment. It is based on his arrogance which tells him that it is his duty to pick the winners and losers of the Treasury Lottery. He is well known for pushing through military equipment, to be built in his district, which even the Defense Dept. claims is unnecessary. But John always knows best; at least according to him.

The majority of his pork is inserted into the Defense Department Budget and most of the projects are of a nature that the Department of Defense neither needs, wants nor sees the value of. But they go through because Pennsylvania, and especially the Johnstown area, is carpeted in defense contractors. In a position of power as the Chairman of the Defense Appropriations Committee he is the open door by which winners and losers are ushered in and out of the system.

When recently questioned by a reporter on the method of disclosure, now required by the Transparency and Accounting Act, of his earmarks, and the methods he has fashioned to make it virtually impossible to reconstruct money and projects he sponsors, his response to the reporter;

"So you have to work for a change, Tough Shit."
(I guess that's Congressman talk for "you lazy bastard")

It is difficult to believe "change we can believe in" when you have this level of arrogance, self importance and incumbency protectionist thinking and beliefs that so directly display the belief that Honesty,

Integrity and Ethics" have no home in American politics today. Obviously Rep. Murtha has left a trail of misappropriations, campaign finance violations and theft of the Treasury across the 34 years he has been in public office and to cover it all really requires its own book because it is more extensive than can be handled here in one chapter, but we'll try to hit the most egregious.

They call it "Murtha's Corner" where you go when you need to protect your incumbency, payback your special interests and supporters or need someone who can make a silk purse from a sow's ear." In a position of power as Chairman of the Defense Appropriations Committee his is the door by which the contents of the Treasury are doled out to those who "play the game, become a piglet and vote the way they are instructed." You need only check your ideas of ethics, morality and honesty at the door.

It's where Murtha and his band of pink piglets decide the winners and losers of the Treasury Dept. lottery that exists today. Never mind the fact that the Constitution and subsequent rulings by our Founding Fathers expressly deny the use of Treasury Funds to benefit one state over another or support of individual companies or industries at the expense of others. Murtha has never met a pig he wouldn't mate with or a Constitutional provision he was not willing to ignore. Unfortunately too many of our politicians today are willing to sacrifice honest politics for self protection. Greed and the tentacles of corruption have encircled too many to count and serious disciplinary solutions and honest ethics violation investigations are the only tool for rooting out the evildoers of this system.

Some facts and figures of "The John P. Murtha Regional Airport" perfectly illustrate the process of Rep. Murtha when it comes to looking out for his future. Now approaching $200 million in special earmarks, just what exactly are we getting for this money?

The anchor tenant of this airport is a unit of the Pennsylvania Nation Guard which, according to Murtha, required a runway large enough to support the largest of military aircraft. In addition they required a $14 million dollar hanger training center and an 8 million dollar radar system which was completed in 2004 but has yet to be used. Interestingly enough this was not a new unit of the National Guard but one already based in Pennsylvania just not in Murtha's district.

And that runway that had to be able to handle the biggest aircraft the military operated? Well surprise! This unit flies only helicopters. What was wrong with the airport they previously occupied or the runway that already existed at the Murtha airport? But wait it gets even better!

This airport also serves as a commercial operation, much needed in his district, but the statistics have to make you question the value of our money going into this airport. With 6 flights per day in and out, which if extrapolated over 10 years, shows that it costs taxpayers $25,641 per flight. Servicing a county with a population of 152,589 residents we have spent $1,307 per resident to support this airport which serves less than 10,000 passengers per year at a cost of $1,282 per passenger over 10 years. But wait, there's more! Because the airport doesn't generate enough operating income to break even, we also subsidize its operation at $100 per passenger in and out for ten a year total of $15,600,000. Another interesting fact is that 3 of these daily flights are to and from Dulles International Airport. A matter of convenience to the "Big Murtha" or does everybody in Johnstown vacation in Washington D.C.?

In December 2008 Murtha requested $800,000 for resurfacing of an alternate crosswind runway, which the FAA turned down because it didn't meet the minimum requirements.

Then enter the stimulus bill and Murtha found his way around the FAA. Because it is stimulus money the project was inserted into the bill and the FAA gave it its nod of approval. I guess it's okay because it just isn't real money!

Described by Steve Ellis of Taxpayers for Common Sense as "practically a museum piece" the one thing we can be sure of is that we haven't seen the last of our Treasury funds being wasted on this monument to self aggrandizement and political payoff.

With known and established relationships with lobbying and defense contracting firms employing or owned by relatives, some even owned by convicted drug traffickers, several currently under investigation by multiple departments of the government for illegal campaign contributions, with money moved from one company to another to try to hide the original source; Mr. Murtha is tied to so many government investigations that it probably wouldn't even be possible for Mapquest to lay out all of the tentacles of his corruption.

From support for the construction of shiny new buildings for companies who received millions in Defense Contracting but never occupied these buildings, to Defense Contractors with offices in his district, commercial business parks bearing his name and offices obviously no more than a sham but established with minimum personnel simply to give them an address in his district, literally billions of dollars have been funneled from our Treasury to his political supporters, special interests and the "Murtha Family Trust Fund." The Murtha system of government is about looking after your own at the expense of everyone else. No shame, no degradation nor actual embezzlement of Treasury Funds can stand in the way of nepotism, self interest and payback of political debts.

Described as nothing more than a "walking talking ethics violation" I think the next earmark we should all get behind is one that would be used to construct a "Murtha Friends and Family Wing" at the Pennsylvania State Prison. That way he and his family members as well as lobbyists and favorite defense contractors could all be together.

I think he'll look good in pinstripes but you watch; he will probably demand a prisoner number in the millions if for no other reason than just out of habit!

Chapter 17

Good enough for you but not good enough for us!

So many committee meetings, bludgeoning of key players in the financial world and the cry for reform against CEO's and others, Congress cried that these CEO's had to have some skin in the game. If they didn't then the support of our government was going to lead to misuse and the rewarding of the very people that caused the implosion of our financial system.

It all sounds so good to us; finally Congress is really looking out for us. But, are they really?

Within 2 days of the final take over of GM creating Government Motors, swearing the whole time that Congress was not going to be involved in the running of the new auto company, Rep. Barney Frank placed a call to the CEO of GM advising him that it was not in the best interest of Rep. Frank's district to have them close a parts warehouse which employs 93 people. The result of this conversation was that the warehouse was kept open and another warehouse in somebody else's district closed. In other words Rep. Frank made sure that his district had no skin in the game. If you were the recipient of that call how would you respond?

Stating that he only did what any responsible Congressman would do to protect his district he declared, "it was just a case of me doing my job!" So we have to infer that anything he chooses to do under the powers of his position are justified and beyond reproach. Involved where he stated members of Congress wouldn't be, exercising powers where inappropriate and making decisions that benefit his district are above reproach. To me it has the scent of ruler not representative.

And then there is Senator Grassley displaying the attitude of the members of Congress in its "truest form" displaying the true problem in Washington, the attitude of entitlement.

Over the 4th of July weekend he held a town meeting in his home state where confronted by a constituent who asked why we couldn't have the same health care coverage that Congress and government employees enjoy. The response was a condescending chuckle and the answer that "…you will never have the same coverage we have unless you run for and win elected office or go to work for the government!" A portrayal of the true lack of respect for the interests of those they are elected to serve. No longer representatives but rulers who feel that they are entitled to have everything even that which they would deny the people who elected them.

While they are not close to agreement on Reform they took care of what they consider to be the most important issue of the bill; making sure that the provision "excepting themselves and employees of the Federal Government" was put into the first draft.

This is our leadership at work. As hard as I look I have real trouble finding signs of this "New Era of "Responsibility." There is just simply no evidence in actions, words or deeds.

Remember these attitudes and the flimsy excuses of why they are so much more entitled than the people who are paying their salaries as well as their personal political debts. As you read through the examples of *"Pork Barrel Spending"* which found its way into the stimulus bill as well as the general budget ask yourself; how much of this money, rather than being misused the way it is, could have been used to give us true Health Care Insurance reform?

Remember the words of Senator Kennedy who I think got it right when he said "health care reform won't be complete until everyone has the coverage we have." I wonder if Senator Grassley has ever heard Senator Kennedy speak? He was probably back home that day laughing in the face of another unemployed, uninsured constituent who has cancer or is trying to save his house from foreclosure! To him I guess it's funny how some of us just get in over our heads.

Chapter 18

Pork Barrel spending: Embezzlement by any other Name

Embezzlement means to "misappropriate or direct fraudulently to one's own use." See if the process doesn't meet the definition.

We all know them as "earmarks," those pesky expenditures which typically have no author attached to the bill, have no debate within the Congress and are generally for projects that none of us can understand. However the real terminology should be "Pork Barrel" spending.

Earmark is a term which should be reserved for the identification of funds that are specifically tied to a particular account in the budget. For example: Social Security funds are those monies collected through our payroll withholdings which are dedicated to the Social Security fund, gasoline and highway use taxes are earmarked for the Federal Highway Fund.

The actual term "Pork Barrel" spending identifies those funds for pet projects of our legislators such as "Swine Odor" research and the "Bridge to Nowhere." Pork Barrel is a specific Congressional provision which is used to direct funds, specific tax exemptions or mandated fees to a specific project, person or corporation. Forget the fact that it is a direct violation of the Constitution for now. They are the currency of political capital. If we were talking about a public corporation it would be identified as embezzlement.

It is a system based on "political muscle' rather than "merit" and is all too often used to pick the winners and losers of the government lottery whereby protecting the interests of clients represented by Lobbyists is the first and only order of business. Their first defense is always that "pork doesn't increase government spending" which is very true. What they don't admit to you is that the money is being re-directed from another government program without determination of the merit of the victim program versus the "Pork Project." It is at the sole discretion of the member requesting the funds.

Probably the most obvious understatement so far by the new administration;

> "On occasion earmarks have been used as a vehicle for waste, fraud and abuse. Projects have been inserted at the 11th hour without review and sometimes without merit."

Did he really say sometimes? Think about the decision on September 30, 2009 by the leadership of Congress that they would not post the Healthcare Insurance Reform Bill online for scrutiny by the public. Why is that you ask? Because they don't want to make available to us the opportunity to see the billions in "Pork" already inserted into this bill. When you want to hide something you certainly can't make it public!

"The Bubblegum Committee!"

To really understand how they use their Pork think of a bunch of kids sitting in a circle trading baseball cards. True they don't come with bubble gum, but with the billions of dollars they are trading back and forth they can buy their own bubble gum!

This simple lack of oversight enables politicians to "bring home the bacon" as they say for pet projects, personal campaign contributors and/or their businesses, reward lobbyists who grease the wheels of reelection and protect incumbent politicians facing difficulty in their next election cycle.. In other words the lack of oversight opens the door to corruption by the very politicians that are supposed to be protecting our societal interests not the interests of the few or the special interests.

I believe that the proper definition, and I think you will agree, is the behavior of Rulers not Representatives.

They are also widely used as bargaining chips between politicians to get support for their bill when another politician might be inclined to vote it down. You scratch my back I'll scratch yours. That is how we end up with 3.5 Billion dollars being paid for a single yes vote on the Cap and Trade Energy Bill.

It's about the powerful in Washington raiding the Treasury to increase their power and influence. The power comes through membership of the Appropriations Committee's from chairman down to the newest member. The "Bubblegum" committee members perform the back and forth trading necessary for protecting the interests of the few over the good of all. It is the practice of redirecting taxpayer money directly from the Treasury into "purely political purposes."

A little known fact that is never discussed in the open is the unintended consequence of more money poured into the wealthier districts than into the poorer areas.[28] It is inadvertent racism by its very process. Representatives from the poorer districts rarely experience difficult re-elections therefore require and receive little money to protect their incumbency. These Representatives lack the high powered committee positions which allow control of the purse strings and the political alliances necessary to get their fair share of the spoils.

"…distribution to white versus minority members, there is a clear disparity. Of 4.2 Billion Dollars in earmarks sponsored by individual members and included in bills for the Fiscal Year that began Oct. 1, 2008 white Democrats averaged a total of $12 Million per member in special projects while black Democrats, on average, a bit over $6 Million per member. The average of Hispanic Democrats is a bit less than $6 Million per member."[29]

Prior to the passing of the "Federal Funding Accountability and Transparency Act" signed into law on September 26, 2006 the process was set up to avoid

> Public debate
> Open bidding Process
> Re-direct spending
> Subvert state, county and city application of review process
> Lacked identifying information in order to hide the identity of the author and the beneficiary of the funds

---

28   CAGW "All about pork: The Abuse of Earmarks and the Needed Reform"

29   CAGW "All about pork: The Abuse of Earmarks and the Needed Reform"

This bill was an attempt, presumably for public appearance, of changes in the way business is conducted. It was meant to bring the system into the open removing the tradition of secrecy and lack of responsibility. But as with most things politicians do there is always a back door left open to circumvent the system. And there seems to be no shortage of "doormen" available to assist their sneaking in.

January 29, 2008 then President George Bush signed an Executive Order that put limitations on the funding of pork contained in committee reports or other non-statutory sources. Current practices are not based on law but rather the cooperation of your fellow legislators. On September 24, 2009 the House passed the 2009 fiscal year Defense Authorization Act which included over 50 billion dollars in pork. According to the Executive Order these pork projects could not be funded because they had no basis in law. To circumvent the Executive Order Chairman Carl Levin simply put into the bill language that gave the included pork "the force of law" thereby neutering the Executive Order and taking care of his and his colleagues special requests.

Why did they write this language into the report at the last minute; because eight months was "...just not enough time for them to insert their "pork" into the statutory language?" Was there concern for the way they circumvented the Executive Order? None what so ever, because where there is no accountability there is no fear.

The attitude of Congress is if there are rules or laws against it then just change them to fit your needs or circumvent them all together. Changing the rules under which amendments can be introduced on the floor for debate the Democrats have effectively shielded themselves from having to vote on amendments to the Health Care Insurance Reform bill and preventing Republicans from introducing amendments to the bill. So the spirit of bi-partisanship is really nothing more than a smoke screen meant to hide reality from the public. Congress rarely passes a bill restricting their behavior without leaving themselves a hole in the firewall.

A Conference Committee Report is the result of lawmakers from both the House and Senate, usually made up of ranking members of the committee putting forth the original bill, to iron out the final language of a bill after it has passed both houses of congress but contains different language. It is at this point where most of the trading goes on. If they insert the pork into their *conference committee report* it guarantees passage because the report cannot be challenged by amendment or debate on the floor of either house of Congress

The use of Pork Barrel spending is a distortion of the best ways to spend our money because the money had to come from another budgeted program. They use the backdoor to approval because they know that debate and explanation can not hold up to public scrutiny.

They passed the transparency bill but still lack the discipline or inclination to follow the law. Evidently these laws are meant for others. I guess following the law can sometimes be inconvenient! Thus they do it behind close doors and hide it from the public. They insert them into bills at the last minute so that there is no possible chance of debate on the floor of the House or Senate.

Perhaps Senator Harkins' now infamous swine odor amendment would have been unnecessary had he simply stepped back into the chamber of the Senate and taken a deep breath through his nose he would have found the real source of this noxious odor. Problem solved, that will be $1.8 Million please. Lest you should feel bad for him rest assured he got the money.

Ask yourself; what is Sen. Ted Stevens from Alaska best known for? What is his definition of how successful his career in the Senate has been? It's all about the Pork he has returned to Alaska! Also, remember that he was not acquitted of the charges in his trial at the end of 2008, but rather it was dismissed because of the blatant abuse of facts by the attorneys of the Justice Dept. But he isn't the only one, I have devoted entire chapters to some of the biggest violators showing the abuse and how they glorify themselves in the process.

Regardless of how the elected officials view it, it is still our money! We as taxpayers are the contributors that make up the total pie and yet our elected officials think we are too stupid to understand and make determinations of how that pie should be divided. But maybe their impression is correct; after all we keep returning them to positions of power. We continually accept deception as the norm. It would seem that we as the governed have bought into the politician's belief that they are Rulers not Representatives.

Chapter 19

In his own words!

"Throughout America's history there have been years that simply rolled into the next without much notice or fanfare. Then there are years that come along once in a generation, the kind that make a clean break from the troubled past, and set a new course for our nation.

This is one of those years."[30]

Other campaign promises

"Now the very fact that this crisis is largely of our own making means that it is not beyond our ability to solve."

"It is time to trade old habits for a "New Era of Responsibility." It is time to finally change the ways of Washington so that we can set a new and better course for America.

"Instead of politicians doling out money behind a veil of secrecy, decisions about where we will invest will be made transparently and informed by independent experts wherever possible."

"…our goal is not to create a slew of new government programs, but a foundation for long term economic

---

30   www.usnews.com/articles

> growth. That also means an economic recovery plan that is free of earmarks and pet projects."

> ."…this must be a time when leaders in both parties put the urgent needs of our nation above our own narrow interests."

> …"sign no bill until it had been posted for sufficient time that all can read it."

These are direct quotes from President Obama's speech on his American Recovery and Reinvestment Plan delivered January 8, 2009.[31] There was also a promise that he would sign no bill until it had been posted for sufficient time that all could read it.

It all sounds good and this is not an attempt to denigrate the President's performance thus far. We can all agree that it is much too early to draw conclusions on his ability to change the way government does business. It is however important to note differences in promised goals and reality of actions.

With over 30 Czars now filling what are largely new departments of the government it is hard to argue the case that "…slew of new government programs" is being seriously monitored. There has been a huge increase in the number of departments as well as the number of government employees. The Federal Government is almost the only employer still hiring. But you can't lead the economy out of recession by increasing the size of government.

You might also have difficulty seeing the interest of our nation versus the interests of our legislators in their own personal pet projects. Supposedly the end of Earmark and Pork Barrel spending, spending decisions made behind closed doors and changing the ways in which Washington does business were little more than pipe dreams.

It is interesting when you look at the entire process just how feeble our legislator's excuses are for their poor performance. While they all cried out about not having the time to read the bill before they were required to cast their vote, there was sufficient time for them to write

---

31 www.usnews.com/araticles/news/stimulus/2009/01/08/president-elect-barack-obama

their funding requests for pet projects which, in almost all cases, benefit only the requestor and are used as a way to strengthen their position at home or to pay back political debt.

In more than half of them you will find it difficult to find any jobs created or saved. You will be amazed at how your money has been spent. And you will come away with a sense of wonder about the benefit to us of all of these pet projects. You may even be like I was after researching these earmarks and question who in the name of God thinks up these projects and is able to justify their importance with a straight face.

Projects such as Senator Patty Murray's, my state's Senator, study on the benefits of smoking marijuana in conjunction with the use of morphine really helps. Are you kidding me? Is the answer to the question "to smoke or not to smoke" with our Morphine really worth $148,348? Sounds to me like one of our most pressing issues. How about you? You may think it an anomaly but oh how wrong you would be. It is down right scary, as you will see, how they are able to spend our money.

While it is unfair to criticize the President for his inability to change Washington in a few months, you do have to question why a bill that was suppose to be "Pork Free" was allowed to pass and be signed by the President especially given all of his statements to the contrary.

And now we are in the run-up to the Fiscal year 2010/2011 budget and a new flu season and we still have no vaccine. God help us!

Chapter 20

And Now We Have The Stimulus Bill!

"I sincerely believe…that the principle of spending
money to be paid by prosperity under the name of
funding is swindling futurity on a large scale.

Thomas Jefferson

Another case of speed equaling waste, the Stimulus bill was rushed through as a must have in the next two weeks to protect our economy from sliding further into recession. Like so many of the bills rushed through Congress between September 2008 and June 2009, the Stimulus Bill further evidences the fact that our Legislators suffer from *"Congressional Alzheimer's"*. With all of the waste and supposed corruption of our bank bailouts, the fact that none of them even read the bill before it was passed and the language inserted into the bill, by Sen. Dodd, again that nobody even read, couldn't we have slowed down enough to at least make the Stimulus Bill meaningful and, God forbid, "pork free?"

It was slowed down only long enough for the House and Senate to infect it with the "Swine Flu." With over 100 separate pork projects totaling over $5.5 Billion this bill should have been forwarded to the Center for Disease Control for vaccine injections prior to being unleashed on the public. The old saying "haste makes waste" couldn't be more true just as "you can't teach old dogs new tricks" is the perfect anecdote to describe our elected officials. Rare is the bill that doesn't come out of committee shrouded in a pink coat and sporting a curly tail.

Sen. Harkin more than anyone else was able to grasp the true "scent" of the bill when he put his mark on the stimulus requesting the now infamous $1.8 Million for his *"swine odor"* study. My first thought here is that he got to close to Sen. John Murtha's' *"corner pigpen"* which is probably the true source of the odor. The prolific Sen. John Murtha whom has never met a pig he wouldn't mate with has in fact given birth to so many little piglets that I have devoted an entire chapter to his "breeding enterprise!"

Waste, Abuse and Fraud

According to his own estimates, Earl Devaney newly appointed head of The Recovery Act Accountability and Transparency Board, *"we can be assured that of the $787 Billion total of the Stimulus Bill at minimum there will be $55 Billion, or 7%, that is lost to waste, abuse and fraud."* But that figure does not include the estimated $5.5 Billion in pork nor the billions that will be wasted on projects that are not job creation projects or the projects that will be years in the starting phase. *Nor does it reflect increased public subsidy dollars that will be required in additional benefits for the high unemployment rate while we experience shrinking revenue's coming into the treasury!*

What could these wasted billions be used for now? How about another 153 weeks unemployment benefits for the over 6,000,000 unemployed in the country, many of whom have run out of benefits? Why not hire 1,375,000 new teachers at $40,000 per year or 500,000 new teachers whose salary is covered for the next three years? You could hire 1,100,000 new police or fire personnel or again, 500,000 and have their salaries covered for the next three years.

There are a lot of ways this money could be spent for the overall good of society but our politicians seem to be okay with the potential waste. The sad truth is that $55 Billion is a lot of money! But when you adopt the attitude that $1 Billion isn't worth the effort involved to save it, or the $19 Billion in cuts the President recommended to Congress as potential savings through elimination, wasn't worth the time of review by our elected officials, it demonstrates that we have a serious attitude problem. If you don't earn it yourself money rarely has a true value.

Every financial advisor will tell you that if you need to balance your budget you must first start by reviewing all of your expenditures. By analyzing and eliminating the waste you can start to bring your budget back into balance. Though it is a larger amount of money, the federal budget should work the same way. You have to eliminate waste, fraud and abuse line by line. For us it might be $10 here and $10 there, while the federal budget is $500 Million here and $500 Million there, in the end it all adds up to serious savings.

When you start to go line by line, as President Obama said several times in his campaign, you start to identify and can begin the process of eliminating wasteful, duplicate and unbudgeted spending. Until you are willing to make the commitment as well going line by line, department by department and eliminate the thievery of our Treasury conducted by Congress, nothing will change. And make no mistake about it pork barrel spending is nothing more than thievery. To pull money for their pet projects another department of the government has to give up a portion of their budget without any committee reviews as to the importance of each recipient's program.

It is simply the way that our Legislators make themselves the pickers of winners and losers rather than the merits of the various programs to society and open honest bidding determine the winners of the Treasury Lottery..

The saddest thing about the Stimulus Bill is the fact that President Obama stated he would accept no pork in the Bill, but when it arrived on his desk he failed to make good on his word. Regardless of whether you are with the Republicans or the Democrats, approved of or objected to the Stimulus bill, had the Democrats not turned it into an opportunity for free wheeling spending for their personal agenda's, it would have been more palatable to the taxpayer. The real winners here are the politicians coming up for reelection in the next few years as well as the lobbyists and special interests.

When playing Monopoly, as in real life, the winner is usually the player who takes Stewardship over their money and the losers are the players who treat their resources as make believe money. Until we start to put Legislators into our Government who know the difference between our money and Monopoly money there is no hope.

With more than 100 pork projects included, the Stimulus Bill can be called a lot of things but never "Pork Free." The following are examples of the dubious projects which mysteriously made their way into the bill evidently unnoticed by those voting on the bill and the

President who signed the bill into law. We have a serious problem when our representatives don't take the time to read a bill before they vote on it. Couple that with an administration which always wants things done yesterday and you have "A Perfect Storm" of waste, abuse and fraud that could bankrupt our country.

With help from Oklahoma Senator Coburns' report on Stimulus Bill Pork report and the 2009 Pigbook of Pork in the fiscal year 2009 budget published by Citizens Against Government Waste the following projects are broken up into sections meant to question their value and the net effect of their implementation.

Chapter 21

FutureGen; Defined to be a Clean Burning Coal Plant Instead Smells Like Barbequed Pork!

Originated when President Obama was Senator Obama and Rahm Emmanuel was Senator Emmanuel; it is a project whose time never really came but for sure is now a relic of the past. Inserted into the Stimulus bill it now becomes the biggest single pork project in history. It would appear that Chicago style politics are at play here.

Now you see it, now you don't, oops there it is again! Perfect slight of hand brings this project back to life some 6 or 7 years after it was first touted as an "experimental clean burning coal plant." It is the perfect example of political game playing which goes on daily behind the cloak of secrecy in our government. And if you think it doesn't reach into the White House read on.

A public/private project which sees the government paying for more than 70% of the total costs of this plant it was first floated in 2003. For the next 4 years there would be more some 20 million dollars spent by the coal industry lobbying Congress along with some 3 million dollars donated by the alliance of public companies that will benefit from the public/private relationship of this plant. The state of Illinois spending over $460,000 on lobbyists of its own to help them win the site location battle going on between itself and Texas.

Some say that in 2007 when the Mattoon, Illinois site was chosen over two sites in Texas then President Bush began working behind the scenes to kill the project on the basis that it would be utilizing unproven technology, soaring costs doubling the final tab and the imbalance of taxpayer money to private monetary participation. Legitimate reasons?

Probably. Definite political abuse behind the scenes? Almost certainly. Politics as usual? Absolutely.

As recent as last year, then Secretary of Energy Samuel W. Bodman stated that "FutureGen was announced in early 2003 as a $950 million initiative to create a single coal based power plant where new technologies, then revolutionary, would be demonstrated. Since then the project's estimated cost has almost doubled and innovations in technology along with changes in the marketplace have created other viable options for demonstrating carbon capture and storage on a commercial scale. ..it became clear the Department of Energy could not, in good conscience, continue to support the program. The likelihood that it would fail, leaving the American people with hundreds of millions of dollars in sunk cost and none of the benefits, is not acceptable."[32]

Following the Bodman announcement that the project was dead Senator Durbin, in a heated meeting in his office with Secretary Bodman and other Congressional backers of the project is quoted as saying "we won this competition fair and square...we are going to keep this alive for the next president."[33] And so they did!

In spite of a 2007 study performed by Massachuset Institute of Technology which determined that the project was a waste of money and lacked clarity of objectives for the program Senator Durbin, true to his word, kept hope alive. The study's recommendation was that the government should look at a portfolio of smaller projects rather than being singularly focused on just one project.[34]

One of the first meetings of the new administration, an orchestration of the slight of hand necessary to perpetrate this project without appearing to be the driving force, set the stage to bring it back to life. Although the President announced that he would not sign the bill if it "included the FutureGen project" and Brendan Daly, spokesman for Speaker Pelosi's office, verified that "it was Obama's decision to exclude

---

32 New Technology makes FutureGen a waste of tax money" Then Secretary of Energy Samuel Bodman 2/6/08

33 www.washingtonpost.com/wp-dyn/content/article/2009/03/05/

34 http://web.mit.edu/coal/The_Future_of_Coal.pdf

the funding and that the speaker had ensured that it would not be in the Stimulus Bill, it magically appeared in the final bill.[35]

Evidently in Chicago politics there are two definitions of serious; the first is that you definitely remove the subject of your statements and the second being that you give the appearance of its removal under a smokescreen of changing language to vague and undefined purposes. Either the Administration, like congress, no longer has time to read the contents of a bill, even though they have hundreds of staffers, or they struggle with the meaning of the English language.

With five simple words "fossil energy research and development" inserted into the 400 pages of the Stimulus Bill, FutureGen was not just given new life but also a billion dollars of seed capital. This language makes it appear as though there can be many projects submitted under this classification but in reality it is a thinly veiled slight of hand because FutureGen was the only proposed project in existence which could meet the definition.

So five little words cost the American Taxpayers 1 Billion dollars for a project that will cost over twice that much, meaning we have only made a down payment with this first billion, to fund a project of dubious value by most in and out of government, including the best minds MIT has to offer, for a project that while supposedly being a public/private partnership with the government paying the majority of the cost while benefiting the private sector in a bill which is supposed to be "PORK FREE."

They expect us to listen to them and trust that what they say is "the truth, nothing but the truth so help me God" but continually show us that while preaching to us from the left side of their mouths they are whispering among each other from the right side

---

35   www.politico.com "Obama Team Wants Earmarks out of Stimulus"

Chapter 22

Stimulating Pork

Shouldn't you have kissed us first?

The jobs were already created, the project financing in place, preliminary cost estimates prepared and the bidding process was ready to go public. So what happened?

Here we have a project ready to go, already creating jobs with everything in place including the agreement of the local residents to tax themselves with a 60% increase in their utility bill to repay the financing. So you would think with the "FREE" stimulus money reducing the costs to the utility it would enable repayment of the loans to happen much sooner than originally planned and the rate increase being paid by the residents would be removed even sooner than planned. So what really happened?

Whenever something comes from our government with the moniker of "FREE" there will be strings attached. After all there are political supporters to be repaid. So how does the government math really affect this project?

It's the Stimulus Bill to the rescue and Perkins, Oklahoma do we have a deal for you! We are giving you 1.445 million dollars to help you build your new wastewater treatment plant. Now anyone with even the most rudimentary of mathematical ability would subtract the "FREE" money from the original estimate of 5.26 million dollars and come up with a total out of pocket cost of 3.815 million dollars to complete the project. But that isn't the way government math works!

The original cost estimates for this project were 5.26 million dollars and the government gifted them 1.445 million dollars bringing the total of the project to 7.2 million dollars. Wait a minute you say!

That is really "fuzzy" math! Well yes, but the town of Perkins was now required to use steel or steel derivative materials manufactured in the United States increasing the material cost significantly. They are also required to now use, organized, or union labor.

See if you can follow the government's math!

$$5.26 \text{ million} - 1.445 \text{ million} = 7.2 \text{ million.}$$
(Increase of 27%; "But I thought we were subtracting?")
$$7.2 \text{ million} - 5.26 \text{ million} = 1.94 \text{ million} - 1.445 \text{ million} = \$495,000$$

This results in an unfunded increase to the residents of Perkins, Oklahoma of $495,000 meaning that their self inflicted increase in rates of 60% will have to be assessed for even longer than the original plan.

Is it any wonder the residents are scratching their heads over this government help? I hope they remember to send a huge Thank You card to Congress and the Administration.

I wonder if it has dawned on them yet they weren't even "KISSED" first?

Think it's just money they Make Disappear? Think Again!

Why would we pay the moving expenses for a publicly traded company?

Not according to the people in Dayton, Ohio. You see they had a company called NCR, maker of cash machines and employer of 1200 local residents, but now it's gone! You thought David Copperfield was a great magician? Well he has a few things he could learn from the federal government.

You see, with 5.5 million dollars in stimulus money NCR was able to move their plant out of Dayton to Duluth, Georgia. I thought Duluth was in Minnesota, but this isn't a geography book, anyway, poof an entire company and 5.5 million dollars gone.

Message to Ohio from the Federal Government; don't mention it, we were glad to help!

It would appear that the people of Ohio are *"kissing cousins"* of the people of Oklahoma!

But as someone famous once said, "paybacks' a bitch!"

I guess the Ohio state legislators feel they're even now.

You see they are receiving $774 million and have chosen to overlook several shovel ready projects to redirect 7% or $57 million to planning and preliminary studies for future projects. So at a ratio of 10 to 1 they have taught the government a valuable lesson.

Two highway projects are being studied to the tune of $40 million while another $10 million is going to statewide project planning and a whole $7 million will go toward studies of a proposed Ohio passenger rail corridor. So much for the novel idea of jobs created or saved. Now they can plan all of the future projects that they won't have the money to complete anyway unless the taxpayers stimulate them again.

I have just this one observation; at a cost ratio of 10-1 what I learned is that, unlike in Oklahoma, if you are going to screw the people of Ohio you had better remember to "KISS" them first!

Walking Through the Land of the Idiots! But they must have flown here on our jets.

I can think of 535 people who should be signed up immediately!

Forget the fact that Yale has a 22.5 billion dollar endowment do we really have to give them and Connecticut University $850,000 of taxpayer money to answer for us the age old question; does paying attention really improve job performance and lead to better judgment? I think that there is evidence enough, if you just look at our legislators, to say that there is a true correlation between the two ideas. You really have to wonder how anyone could seriously propose this as a valuable project worthy of taxpayer money.

Perhaps this money would be better spent on a study between the correlation of reading and understanding a Bill before you vote on it.

Excuse me I couldn't understand you.

It must be that accent you picked up walking in the land of Idiots. So even though they have an endowment valued at more than 1.5 billion dollars we just have to give Indiana University $356,000 to figure out if kids have problems understanding people with accents. To you and I it may seem rather obvious but to those lined up at the ATM of the Treasury it makes perfect sense. Sounds to me like these accents are affecting abilities of the researchers in cognitive reason more than hearing problems of children. Maybe they need to take the Harvard study on listening and performance.

Dancing With Idiot's!

Minneapolis Theatre wins stimulus battle and creates 41 jobs while a Solar Panel Manufacturing Company which would have created 360 ongoing jobs gets nothing. Cost of jobs created for the theatre $48,780 per job against Solar Plant cost of $5,565 per job. With the difference of 319 people who will be left on unemployment at $500 (?) per week for the next year it is only costing another $1,914,000 for the next year raising the total waste to $3,914,000. That doesn't even include any other public assistance programs they will need in order to feed their families.

With an unemployment rate hovering around the 8% mark, the Minneapolis City Council must qualify for some special award for ineptitude. I see a new book here;"*Dancing with Dummies for Dummies.*"

Help me I'm drowning!

First of all 1.15 million dollars seems like a lot of money to build a guardrail especially when you take into account that there is already a guardrail in place. But the Army Corp of Engineers says it is a question of "public safety." Okay I am, as you probably are, all for "public safety." But you really have to wonder about the thought process here and what this money could have done.

Optima Lake is located in Guymon, Oklahoma and according to City Manager Ted Graham; "we all feel the county could use a million dollars in a lot better places than Optima Lake...personally, I don't think it should be done." Sometimes politicians get it right and when they do we should acknowledge the fact. You see Optima Lake has never held water. Built in 1960 as water reservoir the lake has never been full. What little water collects in the basin evaporates before it can be used. For 50 years this has been the scenario according to the Geological Society of America.

Is it just a sign of the times?

"Your stimulus dollars paid for this project" signs are like locusts spreading across America. In Illinois alone over $150,000 is being spent to keep us informed. Think about that for a minute; five hundred signs in Illinois alone. Somebody's brother must be a sign maker! IDOT spokesman says "it is difficult to determine how many signs there will be." It occurs to me that IDOT is only one "I" away from idiot.

When pilots get lost at the airport!

Not to be out done, Fort Wayne, Indiana is spending over a million dollars on signs to help guide pilots through runways and taxiways. Now I don't know about you but I think I would get an uncomfortable feeling flying with a pilot who couldn't find his way to the airport runway! Do you really think signs are what is needed most?

Help! We Desperately Need Your Homeless

Union, New York surprised by the receipt of $578,661, like manna from heaven, and were instructed to use it to fight the homeless in their town. Forget the fact that they, by their own statements, don't have a homeless problem. They never asked for the funds and have told the government they don't need the funds. But they still have the money.

Even more for less!

Altoona, Pennsylvania receives even more; $819,000 but they to lack the homeless population necessary to spend this much money. The solution I guess is that we all make a concerted effort to ship them some of our homeless. That's right, every city in the country needs to help Union, New York and Altoona, Pennsylvania. *Please send them some homeless people!*

I am thinking that maybe we need to send out some of the jets in Speaker Pelosi's private air force to pick these people up and fly them in style to Union, New York and Altoona, Pennsylvania. You really have to wonder who decides where the money goes and what kind of statistics they make their decisions from?

It's the age old question; not to smoke pot with your morphine!

Stating that Washington State University is "uniquely qualified to receive these funds because of its potential to stimulate the economy and create or retain jobs within the community." Who sees jobs created in this expenditure? And wouldn't you think there would be an overabundance of volunteers? I would expect that a survey could be done in California where the use of medical marijuana is legal, that would answer any and all questions on this subject.

No "accent" on job creation.

The "accent" would seem to me to be on the waste and lack of jobs creation this $356,000 expenditure accomplishes. It's a study to ""test how children perceive foreign-accented speech compared to native-accented speech." It will also determine how such accents might influence speech development in children. These are supposed to be highly educated people that do these studies; wouldn't you think that they could see the obvious answers to these questions without spending hundreds of thousands of our dollars? If you and I can see it why can't they?

Could diet and exercise possibly have an impact on obesity?

Well Yale University has been given the go ahead to withdraw $680,000 from our Treasury ATM to finally answer that question. What could possibly be the mysterious relationship between these conditions? Are you kidding me? Is this what we want our money spent on? What do you suppose the net jobs created is for this all important study?

Constitutional Restrictions be Damned!

Despite the fact that the Constitution prohibits the spending of Treasury funds to the benefit of private companies, when speed is of the essence, there are no restrictions. At least that is what the members of Congress, who slipped these worthy(?) projects into the Stimulus Bill would have us believe.

Bridges Falling Down, Falling Down!

That's right. With a total of 13,381 bridges in Wisconsin 2021 are in need of repair in some form or another. The first 37 bridges chosen for immediate attention carry a total daily average of 500 cars and are receiving 15.8 million dollars. One bridge averaging 10 cars per day is receiving a $426,000 face lift. Another bridge which services a golf course and a restaurant carries about 260 vehicles a day and is receiving an $840,000 retrofit. These two businesses have got to be excited about winning a lottery that benefits only those businesses. This toll of $8.85 per vehicle for the next year will be completely funded by the American People.

Another Wisconsin bridge which services a recreational area and a private campground is receiving an undisclosed amount even though the Town Chairman Dave Lucey states that "…that bridge is a low priority for us." With other bridges carrying over 60,000 cars per day in need of repair, the definition shovel ready clearly has no relationship with common sense or best use of taxpayer money.

Not to be outdone, Virginia spends $340,000 on a bridge that services 20 cars per day to a gravel road with 7 houses. Even the homeowners question the value of this expenditure.

And the winner is…

The Mayor of Redmond, Washington feeling Microsoft's pain, allots 11 million dollars in stimulus funds to cover cost overruns in the construction of a bridge whose sole purpose is to connect the 2 main campuses of Microsoft headquarters which are separated by a freeway. Though they sit on cash reserves in excess of 20 billion dollars, more than the Federal Treasury has, they need our help? No jobs created because the bridge was already under construction it makes as much sense as spitting in the wind. This mayor read that new book "Political Decisions by Dummies for Dummies."

Are we now bailing out the fishing industry?

Missouri fish farms are struggling to feed their fish. Although it seems as though this should be a normal expenditure of revenue when you make your money breeding and selling fish it is evidently hard to do. So the governor has decided to use $500,000 of our taxpayer money to buy fish food to help these poor farmers out. And I thought farm subsidies were a crock!

Your Government at Work!

They rise from the dead to collect their Social Security Stimulus checks!

Try to imagine, if you can, the consequences of sending out 10,000 checks worth over 2.5 million dollars to people you didn't owe money to. It's reasonable to conclude that in any other corporation in America you would be terminated on the spot and rightfully so.

To the tune of 10 million dollars plus, people dead for 30 – 40 – 50 years received their $250 stimulus checks from the Social Security dept. Factor in the cost of producing a check within our government system and the postage involved to distribute these checks and who knows what the total cost of this boondoggle is. Surely they don't! But if you worked for the Federal Government it would be looked at as the status quo. The responsible people will probably be congratulated for their creativity and promoted upward instead of outward.

1700 Massachusetts Inmates Receive Stimulus Checks

But the Social Security dept. says not to worry because it was only $425,000 and they should be able to recover most of it. Great, but what about the thousands spent to issue and deliver those checks and what about the amount that isn't recovered? The recipients of these checks live where they do because of their upstanding characteristics that will surely make them send the checks back willingly.

I wasn't aware that Canadians were just dying to get into the U.S.

Five U.S - Canada border crossings in Montana received $77 million for upgrades at border crossings. With less than two cars and 3 trucks crossing per day one crossing gets $15 million for renovation. Of course we have to do something to stop the tide of immigrants sneaking across the border from Canada to the promised land. Our elected officials seem to think our immigration problem comes mostly from the North that's why they sent all of the money here rather than to the southern border.

Not to be Outdone Local Governments
Learn from the Federal Government!

Take a look at the Iowa State Legislature!

Many people think that is was good money after bad when Congress and the administration decided to bail out Chrysler and GM. So is now really the time for the State of Iowa to go into the new car business?

Upon receiving 11 million dollars of stimulus money there seems to be a huge lack of creativity in Iowa today. The best and most efficient use of the money has been determined to be the purchase of new state cars. Sounds reasonable? If you factor in the fact that they currently have 48 brand new cars in their storage lot most still having plastic seat wrappers, price stickers and none are licensed do you still think it's a reasonable expenditure? The jobs created shouldn't be to hard to calculate; it should only take two teenagers to wash that many cars each week. Or maybe they have to use union laborers to fill those positions. At $20,000 a piece this is enough money to buy 550 new cars..

They say that new cars lose 20% of their value as soon as they drive off the lot. At 11 Million dollars the net depreciation only comes to $2,200,000 to move them from the dealership to their storage lot.

Paper, Pencils and Backpacks exchanged for
Wine, Beer, Cigarettes and Cell Phones

With $140 million in Stimulus money as well as several million in personal donations the State of New York puts the money out to welfare recipients to the tune of $200 per family to purchase school supplies for the children. A respectable use of the money by most peoples definition. But leave it to the government to take a good deed and turn it to a complete disaster. Remember, the government wants to make all of our health care decisions!

The money was put onto the Debit Cards used by welfare and assistance recipients by the State of New York DSHS office. Simple enough it would seem. But what happens when you do this but don't make provisions for that money going to its intended use of school supplies for the poor? Again, simple enough. It gets spent on wine, beer, cigarettes and other needs of all the poor like cell phones.

It doesn't seem to make a difference whether it is city, county, state or federal government; intelligent thought rarely gets mixed up with purpose. They are able to take the most honorable of programs and turn it into a complete disaster. While they are sitting around sipping their wine, guzzling their beer and smoking their cigarettes what are their kids learning about the importance of education?

How much more of my life am I supposed to spend sitting in traffic?

Forget about teachers, fire and policeman or repairing schools, we have a far greater problem. We all hate sitting in *"rush hour traffic"* but the people of Kalamazoo, Michigan can see the end in sight. With rush hours lasting 10 to 15 minutes per day according to local residents it's only going to cost $43.9 million to expand the freeway so they can get their lives back! Evidently the local officials find the recovery of about 55 minutes per week per driver to be quite stimulating.

Assuming it would take about 500 cars to create a rush hour the total saved minutes per year would equal 130,000 or $337.70 per recaptured minute.

Dishwasher trumps the value of food for seniors

A county in Colorado turns down stimulus money to buy food for senior citizens because once the initial funds were gone they wouldn't be able to continue the program. Changing their mind when the State government told them they didn't necessarily have to use the money for food they did an about face and accepted the money. You will be relieved to know that they purchased an industrial dishwasher and 10 GPS units. If you don't have the food to feed them it doesn't seem to me that you really need a dishwasher. But I can understand the GPS units; obviously these senior citizens are attempting to go over the wall in search of food.

This has to be the Grand Prize winner!

Washington, North Carolina has it figured out! Through a grant originally funded through the Stimulus, they are using the $40,234 that was awarded to them by the Edward Byrne Memorial Justice

Assistance Grant program to hire a "project funding manager" whose soul function will be to find additional Stimulus money for future projects. So we have funded just one job that is designed to figure out ways to get more of our tax dollars for their city. They should win the Grand Prize just for creativity! Is that what the Stimulus is supposed to be about?

What is up in Florida?

As if the hanging chads weren't enough….

Now they want to build a bridge parallel to another bridge less than a quarter mile away. They are going to use 128 million dollars in stimulus funds for a project that is so far from shovel ready that it will probably be years before they can even begin the project, if then. They need to acquire 63 parcels of land for the project and to date have only completed purchase of 33. It is unclear whether they will even be able to come to terms with the owners of the 30 yet purchased. Then there is the question of whether the bridge is even needed since the current bridge is capable of handling the traffic load all but a couple of hours per day. So where will the money go?

Think this is crazy? Read on and you will really question the judgments of this state.

Alligators, Otters and Turtles OH MY!

In Florida they call it the "Ecopassage." What is an ecopassage? Well it's not for you or me but for the swamp creatures that elect to move from one lake to another separated by a highway. I guess the water is always cleaner on the other side of the Interstate.

But lest you should cringe be not worried it's only $3.4 million. Sure it is $2.6 million short of being a shovel ready project but at least we can get a couple designers working on it for the next 5 or 10 years while proponents look for the balance of the funding. With an unemployment rate of 7.3% as of July 2009 I am sure that those people are glad to see how this money is being spent.

Rather than build the "Ecopassage" maybe we ought to build a free soup bar. With specialties such as Turtle soup, beaver stew, alligator and chips and my favorite, swamp creature medley. It would at least feed the unemployed free of charge and cost a lot less than 3.4 million dollars. After all, the ingredients would be available free on the highway adjacent to the soup bar!

The projects major proponent estimates that 9,000 turtles alone have been saved by the temporary fences they installed in 2000. So the project is going to cost 6 million dollars and over 10 years will have saved an approximate 12,000 turtles. The math reveals a cost of $500 per turtle over a ten year period. Surely we can all see the temptation to jump on board this program!

Can your hear the flush?

Remember the $700 toilets they used to buy at the Defense Department?

Well evidently the price has gone up in the past decade. At Somerville Lake, Texas they are spending $11.3 million just to renovate bathrooms and tear down another. This seems like an idea that should be more than circling the drain. It should be flushed entirely.

If you can build restrooms and showers at Black Butte Lake, California for $200,000 why is it so much more expensive in Texas? Obviously because everything is bigger in Texas! Even what they flush

It's only $21,000 a piece

Missouri is purchasing 22 new toilets for $462,000 to replace toilets currently in their National Forest. And Texans thought what they were flushing was big!

Spending Just to spend?

Although $15 million will only rebuild 15 of 42 blocks of the Coney Island Boardwalk the local officials deem it worthwhile because it might, just might mind you, spur further development of the Boardwalk. Coney Island activist, Dianna Carlin, thinks a lot more money is needed if "they want to make this a world-renowned amusement destination." Where will that money come from? Ten to one says it will be more taxpayer money down the road. The popular way of assuring future funds from the Federal Government is to make a partial investment now and ask for more later based on the justification that if the project is not completed we will have wasted the money already spent.

Delaware is spending $7.5 million on restoration of the Rehoboth Beach boardwalk but they will complete the project and hopefully attract tourists to their beaches.

What Good Would Keeping Teachers Do?

Equipment is more important

Rather than bringing teachers back California decides lunch room equipment and technology are more important. Concerned that they wouldn't be able to sustain the teachers once the money ran out they have decided spending the money this way is a better investment.

So $10 million is being spent on non job producing products while various school districts go without special education teachers. Wouldn't it be better to figure out how many teachers could be supported for 3 years with this money? At least then this money would go back into the economy and it would eliminate millions of dollars in unemployment benefits and other public assistance programs.

Don't try to confuse your government with facts

Forget the kids we're thinking cars.

Stating that they have enough pavement residents of a Prairieview public housing development say they would rather keep grass for their kids to play on. However the powers that be in Macomb, Illinois spend $643,945 paving over the grass areas anyway.

Now if we just had some corporate jets.

Hanscom field in Massachusetts gets $3 million for new corporate jet runways even though local officials and residents don't want the improvements saying it is a waste of money and a reward for improper corporate behavior. So who is responsible for pushing the project through anyway?

Lelaunau County, Michigan getting new wastewater treatment plant

Even though the residents don't want or see the need for a new wastewater treatment plant and the fact that local officials can't estimate when this project could be made shovel ready they're getting the $1.3 million anyway.

I guess they don't have unemployed!

Energy efficient street lights and energy audits take precedence over job creating in Rochester, New York. Spending a million dollars on green upgrades rather than trying to put people back to work which would pump money into the local economy plus remove people from unemployment and public assistant programs which cost us all money, makes sense somehow.

What do you mean you don't want it?

Maybe it is the only large green space left around Houston but it's got to go. We've got $181 million to spend and that means a new highway regardless of what the residents say. Plus we also have a developer that wants to come in and develop what is left of the green space after we open it up with a new this new highway. Isn't it always about government thinking they know best?

Do we really need it?

No! But that's not the point. The point is we can get $7 million free from the Stimulus Bill to create new jobs. So we decided we'd use it to build a new government building instead. Sure there is a lot of empty of buildings we could rent, but just think how good this will make us look! I guess Wyoming doesn't have a big unemployment problem.

Forget finding Waldo! See if you can find the jobs.

Ohio Governor doesn't understand the meaning of shovel ready.

Though there are sufficient number of shovel ready projects which would create more new jobs the Governor decides that $57 million of the $774 million should go to research and planning of projects they might like to do in the future. Of course who knows where the money will come from to build them out in the future nor how much their costs will increase it's better to spend it this way than try to create more jobs and get some of our unemployed citizens back to work.

25 police officers will most likely lose their jobs due to funding...

But the governor would rather spend the $57 million on researching and planning future projects. At a salary of $50,000 per year that amount of money would pay for these Columbus police officers for the next 45 years.

Classic Government Reasoning

Due to a history of financial management problems within the Detroit Public School District they are experiencing a $150 million deficit and requiring the appointment of an outside financial manager. And yet the school district is receiving a $530 million from the Stimulus of which $355 million can be spent in any fashion they choose.

Maybe they can get the garbage cans from Rochester, New York.

Decorative sidewalks rather than plain sidewalks, planters, landscaping, decorative lighting, trees and trash cans Michigan, with over a 15% unemployment rate, plans to spend $983,000 on decoration rather than job creation. It will be clear when you get to the Art of Government Waste section.

Aesthetics trump Economics in civic minded Kansas.

Visitor's center pedestrian and bicycle overpass make job creation pale by comparison. The local officials evidently believe that economics are just not as important as aesthetics.

More money on research rather than jobs.

The Army Corp of Engineers plans to spend $2.5 million on beach enhancement studies rather than building projects. It seems with failing levies and dams, beach research should take a back seat.

But I want my own!

A Colorado county sheriff has to have his own new crime response vehicle, like a spoiled child, because the one he currently has access to, when needed, from the Colorado Bureau of Investigation is theirs not his and he just has to have his own! He must have grown up having to share his sister's bike.

Lighting the way to economic recovery?

Wait a minute, I thought it was about job creation. How does installing energy efficient lighting at a cost of $5 million at the San Diego Airport create new jobs? But Transportation Secretary Ray LaHood assures us that it is a "critical investment" that will get the "U.S. economy going again." Really; where are the jobs? How do politicians continually come up with these outrageous explanations to justify waste?

Just a pig on a hog?

Utah county sheriff decides the most important way to spend their $25,000 grant funded by the Stimulus for new equipment can't be spent on anything more important to law enforcement than a new Harley-Davidson! You have got to be kidding!

New technology rather than new police officers?

No new jobs but lots of fancy equipment turns out to be more important to the Phoenix Police Department, they chosen to spend $5.4 million in Stimulus money on equipment regardless of the fact that it was supposed to be used to create new jobs.

Is this why California is in grave financial trouble?

This facelift is more expensive than any Phyllis Diller ever got. Granted skate parks are important to kids but don't they have more pressing needs than a $620,000 skate park facelift? With this kind of decision process is it any wonder they're broke?

Can't we just make some assumptions?

More important than jobs!

Here goes another million dollars that defies the logic of government thought processes. Chicago decides that a study needs to be done to determine whether people living in public housing projects would be healthier if they lived in green housing projects. Of course non of these currently exist but do we really need a study to answer this question?

Did it ever occur to them that maybe the fact that these people are on Welfare, probably Medicaid and other public assistance programs it is more likely that an unhealthy diet is the cause of their biggest health issues? Maybe training them to get off Welfare would be a better expenditure of a million dollars!

There are definitely some strange ideas emanating from Oregon.

Stimulus money is being used by the Bureau of Land Management to study sage grouse flight patterns to determine where we could locate wind farms. It would seem to me, but again remember I am a simple thinker, that the sage grouse are probably smart enough to learn to fly around the windmills. If not it would seem that it is part of the natural selection process!

Just What are They Peddling?

It multiplies out to the equivalent of $11,880,000 per mile!

At $2,250 per foot Eugene, OR must pave their bike trails in gold. This one evidently contains 11,880 ounces of gold. They are spending $2.25 million on a 1,000 foot bike trail. How can this even be possible? It completely defies common sense that it would cost this much. Somebody high up in the state government must have family members in the bike trail construction business!

Milford, Massachusetts gets another $3.5 million

After receiving over $135 million since 1991 for new bike trails only $55 million has been spent. They are sitting on $80 million, or 60% and we're giving them another $3.5 million for. It seems like in

18 years and $135 million they could have completed their trails. You really have to question why the money they have already received hasn't been spent. How many jobs could they have created over the past 18 years with that money?

Bike trails are just cheaper in Massachusetts than Oregon..

At $875,000 per mile Nantucket is spending $5.6 million to repave 6.4 miles of bike trails out of the $473.9 million they received through the Stimulus for highway projects. While it is unclear to me how you qualify a bike trail as a highway at least they're $11 million dollars a mile cheaper than Oregon. Maybe we need to send the Massachusetts bike trail construction company to Oregon!

Rest assured they will be back for more!

In Lexington, Kentucky they are building a 7 mile Legacy Trail from downtown to a horse farm. I thought we weren't suppose to spend money to benefit a private company? But regardless, the $4.7 million they received isn't anywhere near enough to complete the trail but never fear, they will be coming back to us so they can use the infamous ATM machine we know as the U.S. Treasury! Their justification for more money will be that we certainly don't want the $4.7 million we already gave them to go to waste. This is just the way that politicians design their special projects to assure they get everything they want.

With unemployment hovering in the 10% range bike lockers get the nod over jobs.

Portland, OR chooses to build 350 bike lockers in downtown at a cost of $1 million or $2,857 per locker rather than create new jobs. But with this kind of logic I guess they figure that it will provide one locker for each person left employed downtown.

I guess it's an Oregon thing!

Representative Earl Blumenauer OR Democrat wants to throw more money at the failed Capital bikes program believing that Capital staffers will embrace it even though the $23,000 spent over 8 months has been proven to be a total waste. Leasing rather than buying the bicycles $2,875 per month in 9 months the bikes were checked out les than 300 times. At a leasing cost of $766 per bike it has only cost taxpayers $76.67 per use.

The numbers aren't large but it is another example of entitlement and waste by our public officials.

Riding the Waste Train

Choosing museum exhibits over jobs

Dickson, Tennessee decides $200,000 is best used for exhibits in their Clement Railroad Hotel Museum rather than jobs in infrastructure repair. They just want to tell their story.

The voters reject a bond measure to pay for it.

At $233,333 per inch Scappoose, OR is spending $4.2 million dollars to raise railroad tracks at a local intersection by 18 inches to make them level with the street. The 6,200 residents are tired of detouring around this intersection but not so tired that they are willing to pay for it. At $677 per resident it would seem that they should be able to pay for it. It seems like the railroad should have some responsibility here also.

Can't the transit train just quit blowing the horn?

Couldn't they just ask the transit authority to quit honking the horn? Is it really necessary to spend $2.5 million to create a horn free zone whatever that is. Oregon just seems to have a lot of expensive issues with trains.

$25 shovel justifies spending $10 million

Local roads, highways and bridges be damned; we need to renovate this 97 year old train station that has sat empty for the past 30 years. In 2005 the projected estimate costs of restoring the train station came in at 2.5 million dollars. Since then rising costs before the stimulus dollars increased the cost to 4.8 million dollars. With stimulus dollars the cost has now risen to a staggering 10 million dollars or 75% of its original cost and 48% of the most recent estimates. But they say it is justified because they bought the shovel for this shovel ready project over 10 years ago. So they are telling us a $25 expenditure is all the justification needed for this project to move forward. You also have to wonder how this station suddenly became so necessary after sitting idle for 30 years. Without stimulus dollars I bet it loses it's supporters real quick.

Redirecting Funds from Intended Purpose

They turned down the opportunity to create even more jobs.

In Dallas, Texas they want to build a park over a section of freeway. Financing is already in place and jobs were being created then, enter the Stimulus money! With the entire $92.7 million in construction costs already covered by private funds somebody made the decision to redirect $16.7 million in money allocated to transportation projects over to the construction of this park. Funds were meant to cover infrastructure highway projects not the financing of a city park.

Don't the fish need water to swim in?

Fish over water infrastructure projects. Washington State redirects $18 million to growing and hatching fish representing 15% of the allocation for water infrastructure. Who makes the decision for how these funds are to be spent when they were allocated for a specific purpose?.

Dubbed the "train to nowhere"

Alaska redirects tens of millions allocated for mass transit projects to the construction of a train that goes from nowhere to nowhere. With a twelve hour transit time it is hard to believe that locals will be using this train as a commuter train. You'd almost think that Ted Stevens was back but, this time it is Andrew Young who is taking over where Stevens left off.

Weatherization of low income homes takes a back seat

Making the decision for pickups over energy savings they spend $173,824 for new pickups. The money is allocated to a specific project and yet the state redirects the funds. So, while avoiding the intention of assisting 35 low income homeowners to reduce energy costs, have to be satisfied with a ride in a new truck. They also failed to create any new jobs with this money which was supposed to be the goal of the Stimulus.

What the Hell, they're just giving it away!

Sure we had the federal grant of $174,000 to restore our historic train depot in Windham, MA but they wanted us to provide matching funds to get the grant. Stimulus money, provides all of the funds needed and it doesn't require us to use matching funds so it only makes sense that we let the grant expire and take the free money.

They didn't ask for it but they got it anyway

Without being asked by the government the financing for a Chetek, Wisconsin nursing home was switched over from a USDA loan to Stimulus Money to the tune of 2.8 million dollars. City Clerk and Treasurer Carmen Newman says she "doesn't see how project benefited and I don't understand how they can say this is a stimulus."[36]

They not only turned it from a loan, which would generate interest as well as the payback of the principle, to a gift that generates no interest income and in fact we will be paying interest for the money given because we have to borrower it! Will the Administration claim these as *jobs created or jobs saved*? It's hard to see how this could be described as saving jobs.

The Art of Government Waste

Taking Basket weaving 101 finally pays off!

I guess it's a Blue Collar job if there ever was one. Government Arts Jobs in Maine gets $30,000 for basket weavers while storytellers get $20,000. I'm thinking that the storytellers should cry discrimination. And then there is the music festival at $12,500. Maybe it's me that is confused but somehow Maine got the impression that the $1.3 million they got from the Stimulus "are designed to subsidize the preservation of jobs and may not be used for the creation of a new position or for previously unscheduled work."

---

36   Coburn.senate.gov 100 Stimulus Projects: A Second Opinion

I'm thinking maybe these officials need to attend that study on "whether listening has an impact on job performance."

$3.8 million gets you sculptures that are consistent with "Litter Containers."

I feel lucky when my socks match my pants and these guys are creating art that looks like garbage cans! Rochester, New York sees the need to upgrade their Urban Art Trail putting in ground level lighting and putting medallions into the walk. It is hard to figure out just where the jobs will be found in this project but maybe once the new lights are in we will be able to find them.

Government has a definite Comfort Level for Ineptness

History evidently doesn't mean anything.

They spent the money improperly and failed to keep proper documentation of the money but surely they'll do better this time. So we are giving $300 million to these public housing agencies and we'll see how they do. Is this the way to do business? To the government this is a pretty paltry sum so let's roll the dice and see if we get anything for our money this time.

Since they paid their fines before lets give them more.

In violating environmental, safety and discrimination laws CACI International was found to have a history of inadequately trained and screened employees when contracting to the U.S. Army. After their failure to perform we are now contracting them at $1.5 million to help the U.S. Forest Service evaluate projects. Sounds logical if you compare it to the level of competency we get from our elected officials. They are the only ones to whom this would make sense. But maybe they are figuring that we will get our money back through the fines they will levy for shoddy work!

.Didn't they already fire them once?

Okay! In Nevada's defense they terminated the contract with the Community Service Agency who, supposedly specialized, in weatherization of homes for low income homeowners. They realized that these people knew little to nothing of the business they were being hired to cover. But in the interest of speed of distribution for Stimulus funds the total lack of performance by this agency is now acceptable because they were just awarded $1,849,627 of our money in the name of weatherization.

Will it create jobs immediately? Sure. In fact it will create jobs today and a year or two from today when a reputable company has to come in behind them and correct the workmanship. I guess you would have to call that a twofer, except we will have to appropriate more of our money to go back in and correct it. Maybe this is what they mean by the second stimulus. I'm not much of an odds predictor but it sounds to me like the odds are stacked against the house.

You already have broadband?

That's okay take the money anyway. Since 2005 audits show that 90% of the funds allocated through the USDA for installation of broadband services went to communities that already have the systems. Now the Stimulus is giving them another $2.5 billion to allocate to more communities but what makes them think it will go any better this time. It sounds like more of the same. Repeat the same steps over and over while expecting a different outcome.

He must have been kicked in the head!

Rep. Buck McKeon California Republican has suffered some brain damage. I venture the thought that it was one of the mules he wants to honor by spending $50,000 from the Stimulus to study the building of a Mule Museum in tiny Bishop, CA. What more needs to be said!

Chapter 23

If I had 30 minutes to talk with the President...

Mr. President,

You charged the nation with hope. The election was about that hope and because we believed what you said, you rode into Washington on a tsunami of our trust and our expectations that you would fulfill the promises of change which were the focal point of your campaign. Commitments you made to the American people that the Washington insiders were out and the Washington outsiders were now in, that waste and abuse would stop January 20, 2009 and the age of "Transparency" was upon us and would stop business as usual in Washington, D.C.

Perhaps it was our fault that we imbibed you with trust before it was earned thereby lessening its value in your eyes. Things often have less value when they are unearned by the recipient. But we did it, we entrusted our vote to you in the belief that you were different, that you would keep your promises. The performance illustrated thus far can only lead us to believe that you take that trust for granted, that it is your right or due.

The Bush Administration taught us the pitfalls of putting our trust in a "C" student. But now it would seem that we are being taught a new lesson; that ego, arrogance and lack of experience can cause a similar disregard for the people of a nation. It isn't like the Bush Administration set the bar so high, but thus far you appear to not be able to clear it! Our hopes have thus far been dampened by lack of performance and what appears to be an administration that has no connection to the wants and needs of its people. We are weighed down by a sadness of realization that we were duped, that we bought the pitch hook line and sinker.

Ten months into your Presidency we have seen the appointment of people of questionable character to positions of Czar which allows you to circumvent the senate vetting process. Your Stimulus Bill had to be passed so quickly that it was voted on by Congress without sufficient time to read it, even though they had time to insert over 100 amendments of "pork barrel" spending. You promised in your campaign that no bill would be signed until it had been made available for public review and that they would have to be "pork free." Even though you continually claimed no more closed door politics most of your agenda is taking place behind closed doors. You billed yourself as a the one who would finally cross party lines to unite the country, govern from both sides of the isle. But one cross party lines vote does not a bipartisan government make.

The Blue Collar people in this country believed your promise that we would become "the only special interest" of your administration. Thus far however we have seen more of the same; a complete lack of respect for the Blue Collar people, an administration staffed by the same old Washington insiders rather than outsiders, an increase of the lineup at the Treasury ATM for withdrawals of self interests and rather than your new "Transparency" an even more opaque view of government. A significant increase in lobbyists and lobbying within the system since you took office gives real concern to the value of your promises. Instead of fighting the old ways of doing business in Washington you instead focus your energy on trying to freeze out Fox News from the political coverage because they ask questions you are afraid of answering.

It appears as though you have been enjoying your time playing the part of the President but have thus far failed to become The President. You have enjoyed the many perks of the office while more and more people are on public assistance, you make unverifiable claims to such things as "jobs saved" as well as claiming that the Stimulus, still less than 13% injected into the economy, has turned the economic climate around. You push to move a new Health Care Reform bill through Congress but your involvement in creating it has been virtually non-existent, you ignore the people of this Country who elected you, whom have been screaming from the tallest hills in an effort to make their voices heard. You can't continue to spend your time traveling the Country selling your agenda when you have yet to put that agenda on paper, have not been able to prove it would be deficit neutral and have very vague numbers on just how many people would be impacted or what those impacts would be.

Unfortunately this is just the same old claims made by a new Administration. Didn't you say that it was going to different? Didn't you say that it would be the interests of the people that were going to be legislated? You ask us to trust you but look at the promises that have already been broken; the Stimulus was infected with swine flu even though your campaign was all about not signing a bill that contained pork, your numbers on health care have been all over the map and nobody inside or outside government can say just who it will help or what it will cost and you have failed to create your promise of transparency.

From every soap box you could find during your campaign you cried out "A New Era of Responsibility" was on the horizon. But thus far there is little evidence that we are moving toward that horizon. If you are the big hope we all thought you were then it is time that your actions fulfill those hopes. People are losing faith in their government at an unprecedented pace. How come?

Because we have seen this government before; broken promises stacked like cordwood, your party taking more and more indefensible positions on everything from the Stimulus to Cap and Trade and now the Healthcare Reform Bill. It is becoming more and more difficult for the Blue Collar people to invest their trust in you because of the lack of honesty and integrity thus far displayed by your administration. You cry out that we all "just trust you" on Healthcare. That the cost will be paid by savings in Medicare, Medicaid and other government departments to offset the costs of universal healthcare. But how is that different than business as usual? Politicians promise savings all the time but never seem to deliver. Now you want us to believe that your administration is different. How so?

You want real Healthcare Reform? Then show us first how you can save the money, get it all in a big pile and show it to us. Change the laws to rid the system of non-transportability, remove pre-existing conditions and tackle tort reform. Show us that you can do this and I think you would be amazed at how fast the country would rally around you. The American people still want you to succeed but you promised a new responsible and truthful government. Thus far there is little, if any evidence, to demonstrate that you are upholding your part of the bargain. We made the commitment to you. We gave you the opportunity to show us that it could be different. Now is the time for you to step into the position not just act Presidential but be Presidential. You have sacrificed your right to ask us to "trust you" and have put yourself into a position where further trust will have to be earned!

You signed a pork laden Stimulus Bill, Recovery.gov still fails to disclose pertinent information and transparency is completely lacking in your actions so far. Blue Collar people are waiting for you to take your job seriously, get off of television and get to work. You are losing control of your party because you fail to take charge and do what you promised you would do if we elected you. Unfortunately it appears as though we still have more faith in your ability to live up to your promises than you do.

Mr. President please live up to your promises. Quite claiming improvements which are impossible to document, quite blaming the previous administration for all of our problems and stay in Washington to do your job. It does no good to travel the country on the most expensive travel system in existence to sell us on bills that aren't even written yet. Don't ask us to "just trust" you when all you need to do is live up to the promises you made. Fulfill our belief in your potential and we will give our trust.

Thank You for your time.

Conclusion

It is a scary proposition when you look at how little our leaders think of us. But Blue Collar people can't give up all hope. What we can and have to do is raise the bar of expectation. Convert our government back to a "government of the people, by the people and for the people." Quit accepting a behavior from these people that we wouldn't accept from our own children. Insist that honesty, integrity and morals are put back into the greatness of our country. If the leaders can't police themselves then it is our duty and our responsibility to become the police force of fair and balanced government.

As I stated at the beginning, this started out to be a book about the lack of fiscal responsibility in Washington D.C. A look at the self serving ways they spend our money. About the belief that a balanced budget would not be difficult to attain if we just started with the line by line value of our expenditures. But I admit to you that what I ended up finding was an unbelievable lack of understanding as to what the real problems are.

I learned that trust is something we have to be very careful giving when it comes to our government. If we fail to insist that they earn it they will never perceive its true value. The responsibility of monitoring government behaviors is ours and we need to be prepared to demand that all decisions are based on the benefit to all of society. It is time that the American people become not just the "largest special interest in this country, but the only special interest in this country."

Is it attainable? I have to believe it is but it means we all need to be cognizant of the actions of our government, the use of our assets and resources and expend our vote as the weapon against abuse, waste and fraud. I hope that I have reached my goal of providing some thoughts on how we can take our country back and not just demand but receive the appropriate representation and punish those who would rather behave as rulers.

www.ingramcontent.com/pod-product-compliance
Lightning Source LLC
Chambersburg PA
CBHW051415280526
45785CB00003B/1066